ZANE GREY'S

ARIZONA

by **CANDACE C. KANT**

Foreword by **LOREN GREY**

NORTHLAND PRESS FLAGSTAFF, ARIZONA

EB

Text © 1984 by Candace C. Kant
Foreword © 1984 by Northland Publishing Co., Inc.

FIRST EDITION

ISBN 0-87358-354-X
Library of Congress Catalog Card Number 84-60429
Composed and Printed in the United States of America

With the exception of the frontispiece, the photographs and
letter, contract, and dust jacket reproductions included in
this book are from the family collection of Zane Grey and
are the property of Zane Grey Incorporated. We appreciate
the cooperation of Loren Grey and the corporation in grant-
ing us permission to reproduce these items, as well as the
assorted passages from Zane Grey's many books.

FRONTISPIECE: Zane Grey and his horse overlooking the
northern Arizona landscape—the San Francisco Peaks near
Flagstaff, Arizona, are visible in the distance. *Photo cour-
tesy Northland Publishing Company Collection.*

Library of Congress Cataloging in Publication Data

Kant, Candace C., 1949–
    Zane Grey's Arizona.
    Bibliography: p. 177
    1. Grey, Zane, 1872–1939—Homes and haunts—Ari-
zona. 2. Grey, Zane, 1872–1939—Settings. 3. Western
stories—History and criticism. 4. Arizona in literature. 5.
Arizona—Description and travel. 6. Novelists, American—20th century—Biography. I. Title.
PS3513.R6545Z698 1984   813'.52   84-60429
ISBN 0-87358-354-X

CONTENTS

FOREWORD

I am very pleased to have the opportunity to write an introduction to this book, a significant work that explores the very powerful influence Arizona has had on my father, not only as a writer, but personally and as a conservationist and explorer as well. Indeed, as Dr. Kant has pointed out, the image of the American West, which Zane Grey in a sense formulated and which is still accepted by millions internationally, is essentially the result of his experiences and perceptions of Arizona. It is not surprising to know that most of his enduringly popular novels, such as *Riders of the Purple Sage, The Light of Western Stars, Nevada, The Dude Ranger,* and *Man of the Forest,* had their plots and locales based in Arizona. The latter title, initially published in 1918 and re-released in 1977 by Pocket Books, has far outsold any of his novels published in paperback in the same time period. Although the sales of *Man of the Forest,* in excess of 200,000, may seem small compared to the figures for some of the current best-sellers, I feel this is impressive for a book that was written more than sixty years ago.

My father visited and wrote either novels or nonfictional stories about every state west of the Rocky Mountains; however, more than half of his work emanated from Arizona. Though the state lacked only one natural feature that he really loved—an ocean—it certainly had the most incomparable range of unspoiled natural splendor of any place in the world. It is also true that many of the Arizona residents whom he met during his early travels became the living characters who inhabit his books. Tales recounted by pioneers Jim Emett; Buffalo Jones; the Haughts; the Doyles; John and Louisa Wetherill; the survivors of the bloody Graham-Tewkesbury feud in Pleasant Valley; and the many Indian characters, particularly Nasja Begay, who led the first white men to Rainbow Bridge in 1909 and took my father there four years later, served to change many of his own perceptions permanently. My father also took an active part in the lives of these people; he rode, camped, and endured the bitter hardships of outdoor living with them. Indeed, the kind of values they represented—an indomitable will to survive and succeed in the wilderness, a reverence for nature, and a simplicity of moral codes and relationships—became characteristics of the heroes, heroines, and villains portrayed in his books. The contrast between this society, and the complexities and what he came to feel was a growing lack of moral and spiritual ethics present in the industrial and increasingly technological society in which he had been reared, was dramatic. That the eastern literary establishment scorned and mocked these values infuriated him, but did not affect his writing style or the enormous popularity of his books, which endures today.

It is interesting to note that, despite my father's popular successes with the Arizona-based work and his deep affection for the state, he chose California in which to live. I have always known that Arizona was his favorite state, but there were a number of practical reasons why he chose California as his permanent home. For one thing, he discovered Catalina Island as an ideal and easily accessible location that would allow him to indulge his growing interest in deep-sea fishing. He first planned to live in Avalon, Catalina's only settlement, but soon discovered that the cool breezes that tempered the summer heat became very cold and blustery winds during the winter months. He then decided to move to a more protected area of southern California; Altadena, some twenty-five miles northeast of Los Angeles at the foot of the majestic Sierra Madres, became his permanent home. This pleased my mother as well. Though she traveled with him on a number of his early fishing and outdoor trips, she did not feel that the Tonto Basin's primitive wilderness or Phoenix and Tucson's searing summer heat (in those days long before the advent of air conditioning) were conducive to maintaining a home and rearing a family. Additionally, the dazzling lights of Hollywood and my father's involvement with the fledgling motion picture industry made Altadena more convenient for the conclusion of many profitable movie deals.

His final choice for a permanent residence notwithstanding, Arizona provided my father with enormous quantities of material. Dr. Kant has researched and presented a considerable body of previously unknown historical information about his Arizona visits. This should be of great value to both present and future Zane Grey fans and scholars. For example, I think she is correct in pointing out that his decision to finally leave Arizona for good was not entirely motivated by his rather petty quarrel with Arizona bureaucrats who refused to let him hunt bear out of season, but also by his realization that the encroachments of civilization were gradually wiping out the seclusion and isolation that he had so loved about the state. It must be mentioned, though, that leaving the field abruptly when he felt he was losing a battle, or at least not gaining his end, was a personal pattern that he displayed more than once during his life.

Perhaps we should ask ourselves what it was about Arizona and the West that he managed to capture so enthrallingly. One can still see a Zane Grey character in every movie or television western gunman who strides out to do battle with his foe. Recently, a film commentator alluded to the enormously popular *Star Wars* movies as "Zane Grey epics in space." Not too surprisingly, however, literary critics never seemed to understand this, even at the beginning of his success as a writer. Unfortunately, they appear not to have become more enlightened as to why he is so successful today.

One reason may be that most romantic writing—then or now, and particularly with the advent of the *nouveau* realism of the thirties—has never been considered very "literary." In the Dos Passos–Faulkner–O'Farrell era, people had to be mean, vicious, depraved, lustful, incestuous, or victimized by all of the characters who were, to be considered literary. The villains usually won, or else no one did. If one is to measure Zane Grey by these standards, most of his characters would seem to be lacking in the so-called "depth" that the critics demanded.

It is my feeling, though, that one cannot use the same literary yardstick to measure Zane Grey. He was a genuine, self-taught American primitive genius, as were Scott Joplin and George Gershwin in music or Grandma Moses in art. Perhaps the overwhelming characteris-

tic of his writing—whether it be a description of a chilling confrontation
between two deadly gunmen on a dusty western street or his agonies
over hooking and losing a five-pound smallmouth bass—is that he
breathes so much emotional life into these experiences that they seem
absolutely believable at the time one is reading them. On my father's
part, while he was creating them, he loved his heroes and heroines and
hated his villains as much as if he had actually been there with them.
There was so much unexpressed feeling that could not be entirely portrayed that, in his later years, he would weep when rereading one of his
own books.

Finally, Candace Kant has effectively pointed out that the historical
basis for much of his stories was far more accurate than most of his critics, particularly those from the East Coast, were willing to recognize.
With only very few exceptions, they have also chosen to ignore (or
perhaps really do not see) the one aspect of his writing that sets him to-
tally apart from every other western writer who ever lived: his unparal-
leled portrayal of the *soul* of the land, of which I feel Arizona can be
said to be the most representative. The endless, ever-changing vista of
deserts, mountains, trees, roaring rivers, blue-white lakes, or gentle
meadow streams and the accompanying sun, wind, dust storm, rain,
snow, withering heat and body-numbing cold are all part of the Arizona
environment. To illustrate, just a few of these descriptions are given
here.

> Beneath her yawned a wonderful deep canyon, rugged and
> rocky with but few pines on the north slope, thick with dark
> green timber on the south slope. Yellow and gray crags, like tur-
> reted castles, stood up out of the sloping forest on the side oppo-
> site her. The trees were all sharp, spear pointed. Patches of light
> green aspens showed striking against the dense black. The great
> slope beneath Ellen was serrated with narrow, deep gorges,
> almost canyons in themselves. Shadows alternated with clear
> bright spaces. The mile-wide mouth of the canyon opened upon
> the Basin, down into a world of wild timbered ranges and
> ravines, valleys and hills, that rolled and tumbled in dark green
> waves to the Sierra Anchas. [the Tonto Basin, from *To the
> Last Man*]

> Strangest of all rivers was the Rio Colorado. Many names it
> had borne, though none so fitting and lasting as that which desig-

nated its color. Neither crimson nor scarlet was it, nor any nam-
able shade of red, yet somehow red was its hue. Like blood with
life gone from it! With its source at high altitude, fed by snow
fields and a thousand lakes and streams, the Colorado stormed its
great canyoned confines with a mighty torrent; and then, spent
and leveled, but still tremendous and insatiate, it bore down
across the desert with its burden of silt and sand. It was silent, it
seemed to glide along, yet it was appalling. [from *Wanderer of
the Wasteland*]

   At length we turned into a long canyon with straight rugged
red walls, and a sandy floor with quite a perceptible ascent. It appeared endless. Far ahead I could see the black storm-clouds;
and by and by began to hear the rumble of thunder. Darkness
had overtaken us by the time we had reached the head of this
canyon; and my first sight of Monument Valley came with a dazzling flash of lightning. It revealed a vast valley, a strange world
of colossal shafts and buttes of rock, magnificently sculptored,
standing isolated and aloof, dark, wierd, lonely. When the sheet
lightning flared across the sky showing the monuments silhou-
etted black against that strange horizon the effect was marvel-
ously beautiful. I watched until the storm died away. [from
Tales of Lonely Trails]

   Beyond this wide area of curved lines rose another wall,
dwarfing the lower; dark-red, horizon-long, magnificent in
frowning boldness, and because of its limitless deceiving sur-
faces incomprehensible to the gaze of man. Away to the east-
ward began a winding ragged blue line, looping back upon itself,
and then winding away again, growing wider and bluer. This
line was San Juan Canyon. I followed that blue line all its length,
a hundred miles, down toward the west where it joined a dark
purple shadowy cleft. And this was the Grand Canyon of the
Colorado. My eye swept along with that winding mark, farther
and farther to the west, until the cleft, growing larger and closer,
revealed itself as a wild and winding canyon. Still farther west-
ward it split a vast plateau of red peaks and yellow mesas. Here
the canyon was full of purple smoke. It turned, it closed, it
gaped, it lost itself and showed again in that chaos of a million

cliffs. And then it faded, a mere purple line, into deceiving distance. [from *Tales of Lonely Trails*]

These examples serve to reinforce my belief that his writings will endure as long as there are people to read them.

LOREN GREY
Woodland Hills, California

PREFACE

While quite an impressive amount of material has been written on
Zane Grey, most of it either analyzes his western romances as
literature or focuses on narrow aspects of his life. Very little in the way
of either biography or historical treatment of Grey exists, and what has
been produced brushes lightly over the time Grey spent in Arizona. This
book concentrates on Grey's Arizona years and on the literary and
cinematic products of that relationship. Close examination of Grey's association with Arizona reveals the elements that constituted his portrait
of the American West, his conception of its nature and role, and the
basis of his appeal and longlasting fame.

Of prime significance in this study are Grey's novels, which provide
insight into his involvement with the state. The descriptions and settings
reflect his infatuation with the land's physical beauty, while the plots
and themes express the perception of the region that he gave to the
public. The romances were sometimes based on historical events and
figures, and he spent months researching background material, jotting
down notes, interviewing local residents, and visiting locations. This attention to detail and authenticity was often obscured by the fictionalized
romances Grey wove into the historical background, yet much, though

not all, that Grey wrote about western life reflected the reality that he un-covered. This reality, a composite of Grey's experiences, remnants of historical fact, and the influence of the age in which he lived, may be found on the pages of his novels. Indeed, since the novels are the tangi-ble expressions of Zane Grey's Arizona, they are vitally important to an understanding of his association with the region.

Grey wrote many nonfictional articles and short stories that are also important sources of information. The nonfictional articles were pub-lished in such periodicals as *The Country Gentleman* and *The American Magazine,* and, although most have never been reprinted, contain valu-able information about Grey's hunting trips and his thoughts concerning the western wilderness. The short stories contain some of the best of Grey's writing, often overlooked by readers and critics alike. Through these short pieces and the juvenile literature Grey produced, another av-enue for understanding the author's association with Arizona is opened.

Many articles and a few books have been written about Grey. Among these, Frank Gruber's biography, Carlton Jackson's literary analysis, and Kenneth W. Scott's reference guide are outstanding. Richard Etulain's article, "A Dedication to the Memory of Zane Grey," and Danny Goble's article, "The Days That Were No More: A Look at Zane Grey's West," are also of great value. Most of the studies concern themselves with literary critiques of Grey's novels, reviews of the ro-mances, or literary biography, concerned primarily with when and where Grey wrote this or that book; the author's essential motivations for writing the particular piece in the first place are not explored. Valu-able sources of information on the literary aspects of Grey's career, they do little to address the historic role he played as a creator and popularizer of the ideal of the American West.

Correspondence, interviews, newspaper accounts, novels, short stories, and articles reveal the association between Grey and Arizona from which his portrayal emerged. His visits to Arizona were the foun-dation of this relationship and were the most significant source of Grey's impressions. The novels, films, articles, and stories reflect his percep-tions and are a second expression of his ideas, his interpretation of what he saw and experienced, and the effect of the artist on reality. Further, the novels and films contain a third element, the echo of the turbulent world in which Grey lived. A portrait of the Arizona that Grey knew emerges from these sources, and this portrait represents Grey's larger conception of the West.

ACKNOWLEDGMENTS

I nformation on which this study is based was drawn from many sources. The material outlining the trips Grey made to Arizona, including the places he visited, the people with whom he associated, and his reactions to and opinions about the area, was found in private correspondence between Grey and his friends, business associates, and family. Many of these letters were provided for study by Dr. Loren Grey, the author's youngest son, now the president of Zane Grey, Inc. A number of letters were also provided by Reverend G. M. Farley, a lifelong Grey scholar. Quite a few libraries across the United States also possess letters to or from Zane Grey, and access to them for the purpose of this study was freely given. These are the Alderman Library of the University of Virginia, the Arizona Heritage Center of the Arizona Historical Society, the Beinecke Rare Book and Manuscript Library at Yale University, the Butler Library at Columbia University, the Church of Jesus Christ of Latter-Day Saints historical department, the Elmer Holmes Bobst Library at New York University, Colby College Library, Houghton Library at Harvard University, the Horrman Library at Long Island University, the Humanities Research Center at the University of Texas at Austin, the Library of Congress, the Los Angeles Public Library, the Pierpont Morgan

Library, the New York Public Library, the Perkins Library at Duke University, the State Library of Pennsylvania, and the library of the University of Southern California. In all, these sources made available one hundred eighty-two pieces of Grey's personal and business correspondence.

Other sources of material on Grey's association with Arizona were the several specialists who had previously studied some aspect of Grey's life. Dr. Loren Grey, of course, was able to relate many revealing anecdotes concerning his father's experiences in Arizona and other places that he visited. Dr. Grey was too young to accompany his father on the Arizona trips, but many of the incidents that occurred to his father, older brother, and sister on these excursions have become family legends, and he generously related them to me.

Platt Cline, a retired journalist and active historian living in northern Arizona and one who has done an exhaustive study of the history of Flagstaff, made valuable contributions to the project. He helped locate many of the buildings, such as the Commercial Hotel, that were familiar landmarks to Grey. He also provided intriguing character sketches of Flagstaff people like Al and Lee Doyle with whom Grey associated. Also important, Cline allowed access to his collection of original bound copies of early Flagstaff newspapers. Northern Arizona newspapers were rich sources of material. *The Coconino Sun*, (now known as *The Arizona Daily Sun*), a Flagstaff paper published in the early years of this century on a weekly basis, contains accounts of Grey's visits to northern Arizona and the Mogollon Rim. These accounts provided detailed and provocative information concerning the Grey party's itinerary, composition, and purpose. They also covered the activities of the movie crews as they filmed Grey's novels on location in Arizona. Much of the local color and excitement that surrounded the Grey phenomenon in Arizona was revealed in newspaper accounts, and abundant, detailed information was disclosed.

Margaret Sell, proprietor of the Zane Grey Cabin near Payson, Arizona, spent many hours discussing Grey's Arizona adventures and furnished much information about his attachment to the Mogollon Rim and Tonto Basin. She located the actual settings for several of the novels he wrote about that region, as well.

There are many individuals to whom I am grateful for help during this project. Dr. Philip Rulon, Dr. Andrew Wallace, Dr. Leonard Ritt, Dr. Lawrence Davis, and Dr. Margaret Morley have been generous with their aid, time, and advice. Dr. Loren Grey was most helpful in providing material that would have otherwise been unavailable. Funds from the Garland Downum Award made travel to source locations possible. A special thank-you goes to the staff at the Clark County Community College library for their help in acquiring copies of appropriate books and articles. My children, Charles and Caren, and my parents, Charles and Arleene Bull, have my gratitude for their patience and support over the years. Finally, I would be remiss in not expressing my appreciation to my husband James, who has worked with me, comforted me, and encouraged me. Without him, this book would not have been possible.

ZANE GREY'S

ARIZONA

INTRODUCTION

No early twentieth-century American author was as prolific and popular as Zane Grey. Between 1903, when he published his first novel, and his death in 1939, Grey wrote fifty-six western romances, thirteen outdoor books, seven juvenile stories, three historical novels set in the Ohio River country during the American Revolution, one Tahitian novel, and one eastern novel. His numerous short stories and articles have been collected and published in over eighteen anthologies. In addition to his many written works, the fledgling film industry transformed Grey's novels into more than one hundred and thirty motion pictures.[1] This output is given additional meaning by the American public's response to his books and the latest Zane Grey movie. Over one hundred thirty million copies of his novels have been sold, and movies made from his stories have been remade as many as four times. Few exist who do not know the name Zane Grey, particularly among those who were alive during the first half of the twentieth century in the United States, England, Australia, or western Europe. The tremendous extent of his literary activity, as well as the popularity of his work in book and film forms make the Zane Grey phenomenon of importance to students of the American saga. A detailed examination of the elements of his work, particularly the inspiration and sources of his ideas and the factors that made him a success, is vital in assessing the impact of Grey on the American mind.

The portions of Grey's writing most familiar to the public are his fifty-six western romances. These novels constitute the bulk of his work and made his name a household word. Images of hard-riding cowboys, villainous desperadoes, and valiant horses carrying a cowboy and his lady across the purple sage and into the sunset are conjured up by reference to a Zane Grey novel. Through the pages of western romances or in the flickering shadows of a movie theater on a Saturday afternoon, countless audiences breathlessly thrilled to the adventures of the heroes and heroines he created. That most of these adventures took place in the never-never land of Arizona, located in a far southwestern corner of the American West, only added to their enchantment. Over two-thirds of his western romances contain plots based on events in Arizona's past, are peopled by characters modeled after Arizonans, or actually take place in Arizona. With the Arizona novels making up the largest portion of Grey's western fiction, and with the overwhelming prominence of the western novels in his own success, it is curious that researchers have overlooked the significance of Grey's association with Arizona.

Grey became acquainted with Arizona in 1906. From that first introduction, he explored every corner of the territory (and after 1912, state) through numerous excursions, some lasting as long as three months. During these visits he studied the western landscape, researched the history of the region, met the people who lived there, absorbed the atmosphere, and became knowledgeable about the wide variety of lifestyles manifested in Arizona. He took copious notes and collected details on subjects that caught his attention. Using this information and his impressions of Arizona, he wrote romances in a western setting, using Arizona characters, plots, and themes.

These romances are the basis of Grey's portrait of western America. The West had long been endowed with mythical qualities reflecting the nation's concerns; at the same time these qualitites determined attitudes toward the past, present, and future.[2] Grey sharpened America's focus on the nature and function of the West, and added his personal interpretation, addressing it to the issues of the day. From his writing emerged a picture of the West that emphasized the importance of the landscape in shaping the lives and developing the traits of the western personality. His ideas of the West were primarily based upon his experiences in Arizona, and integrated his artistic dramatization and his reactions to the environment in which he lived and wrote. This portrait, with its roots in Grey's relationship with Arizona and its statements concerning the nature and importance of the West, is the focus of this study.

Zane Grey—whose given name was Pearl until he shortened it after he began writing and was addressed as "Miss Grey"—revealed a love of the outdoors very early in his life. Born in 1872 in Zanesville, Ohio, he was the fourth of five children. The family consisted of his parents, Josephine Alice and Lewis M. Gray (the author also altered the spelling of his family name), two older sisters, one older brother and one younger brother. His father was a dentist and wanted Zane to enter the profession, but young Grey was more interested in fishing and baseball. He developed his skill in both pursuits, and his prowess as a pitcher earned him a scholarship to the University of Pennsylvania, where he at last gave in to his father's wishes and studied dentistry. After his graduation in 1896, he moved to New York City to open his practice. For the next several years, dentistry was his profession but fishing was his avocation, and he seized every opportunity to slip away from the office and relax on a grassy bank, pole in hand. By 1902, he had begun to write as well, and published his first article, "A Day on the Delaware," in *Recreation* magazine that spring.[3]

Grey grew up during the time that the theories of Darwin and Spencer were popular in the United States.[4] Darwin's theories developed the concept of evolution of species, and introduced such ideas as the struggle for existence and natural selection. Spencer, in turn, applied Darwin's concepts to human society and coined the phrase "survival of the fittest." Spencer's approach was adopted as the central thesis of many university texts during the period Grey was a student.[5] The controversy over Social Darwinism was a major aspect of intellectual and academic life during the years that Grey attended college. His writing clearly indicates his early exposure to Darwinism and Spencerian theory, in that he paints a picture of a western environment where the struggle to survive and the elimination of the unfit are immutable laws. In Grey's portrait of the West, the harshness of the land was the vehicle through which the process of natural selection occurred. This process, then, created a particular breed of men and women who were strong, fit, and pure. The theories of both Darwin and Spencer thus played a major role in Grey's version of the West.

Grey's younger years, as well, were marked by public idealization and romanticization of the frontier. When he was eighteen years old, in 1890, the United States Census Bureau proclaimed that the United States no longer possessed a frontier line. Three years later, while Grey was still in college, historian Frederick Jackson Turner published an essay entitled "The Significance of the Frontier in American History," which traced America's democratic principles to their origin in the existence of a frontier.[6] Shortly after Grey graduated from college, the United States entered into a war with Spain, and Theodore Roosevelt rose to national prominence. Roosevelt's own idealization of the West, the primitive, and the frontier played no small part in Grey's receptiveness to those themes: his introduction to Arizona and the West came during the years of Roosevelt's administration.

The concern over the disappearance of the American frontier focused on the effect this phenomenon would have upon the nation's values. As the frontier disappeared, Americans attempted to define the role it had played in the development of their nation, and Grey's writing reflected the national mood.[7] No other writer placed the West so squarely in the forefront of his work; Grey gave the western setting great influence over plot and theme, and endowed it with symbolic and restorative powers. He made the West the repository of American values.

Grey shared in the Progressive spirit of the early twentieth century as well. This emphasized nationalism, reform, conservatism, environmentalism, individualism, and buoyant optimism.[8] There was reason to be optimistic, for in the years between the turn of the century and World War I, the United States experienced a prolonged period of prosperity. Technological innovations were heralded as boons to human welfare, and industrialism was thought to be the wave of the future. Thousands of young men and women left the family farm to become urban workers, their numbers swelled by thousands of European immigrants. Some reformers sought institutional changes in an attempt to perfect the economic and governmental systems of the country, while others sought to devise ways to smooth the transition of displaced victims of industrialization and urbanization into the new era.

Progressives endorsed the new urban America, while those with a Populist bent cried out for a return to an older, agrarian society. Both felt that the future of the United States was bright; storm clouds were not yet visible on the horizon. America truly seemed to be the land of opportunity, with no insurmountable obstacles to her progress. Lines of authority were clearly defined and stable, issues seemed simple, good and evil were distinct, humankind was perfectible, and effort was always rewarded. Grey's optimism and faith in the American system and its values sprung from the mood of this age. He retained these values throughout his life, even when events appeared to contradict America's faith in itself.

World War I erupted in 1914, when Grey was forty-two years old. The United States entered the conflict three years later, and the optimism of the earlier period was ended. Americans experienced a sense of despair, doom, and alienation; the seemingly pointless slaughter the war created raised doubts about America's potential for improvement. Optimism seemed out of place in this new era, yet Grey and many of his contemporaries clung to older values and looked back fondly on the golden era of the past.[9] The high point of Grey's popularity—during the period 1917 to 1924—came when America's values seemed the most threatened. His novels appeared in the top ten of the best seller lists every year within that time period, and twice, in 1918 and 1920, his works were rated as the number one best-sellers.[10] Grey's popularity skyrocketed because, unlike many other authors of the time who criticized America, he reaffirmed the promise of the earlier, optimistic years. He urged a return to the traditional values, prophesying that such a return would put America back on the right path. These older values, which he felt were part of the true American spirit, were originally generated on the frontier, and it was there that Americans could still find them. To set the world right again, Americans should look to the West for guidance and inspiration.

Most Americans agreed with Grey, or at least seemed to like what he had to say, and continued to read his work. There was a segment of society, however, that did lose faith in the country. These disillusioned souls fled to Paris or to the intellectual ghettos of New York City, and attacked and ridiculed American culture and values. Many became obsessed with the material culture of the era and indulged in orgies of excess. They flaunted the traditions and the mores of their ancestors, and their frenetic activity named the era. "The Jazz Age," "The Lost Generation," and "The Roaring Twenties" aptly caught the feeling of the times.

Grey's vision of a simpler society, his affirmation of American values, and his faith in the future appealed to many. Throughout the excesses of the twenties and the Great Depression that followed, he continued to endorse, through his writing, the values that prevailed during the opening years of the twentieth century. That he was not alone in this point of view is clear from the popularity of his western novels, in which he dramatized his conception of America's true character.

Grey did not portray a perfect nation. Neither in his novels nor in his personal correspondence did he make the claim that America was fault-less. He acknowledged the despair caused by the war and its aftermath, but attributed it to a loss of vision rather than to any error in the ideals themselves. Like many of his contemporaries, he advocated isolation from European entanglements and elimination of dangerous foreign elements within the United States. He eyed monopolies and huge corporations with suspicion, feeling that they had somehow duped the United States into entering the war. He disapproved of the eastern metropolis and its citizens' materialistic lifestyles, and was utterly horrified by the flapper.[11] He idealized the Anglo-Saxon and attributed all progress, democracy, and hope to that race. While he did not deny the humanity of any other race, he felt that the United States was the unique creation and expression of Anglo-Saxon culture. In a word, Grey was in tune with mainstream American public opinion.

Grey's affirmation of the United States, as well as his criticism, is evident in the Arizona books. The western environment and lifestyle are there, cast as the answer to the country's problems, a model to emulate, and the ideal that Americans should cherish. In the West, Grey contended, it was possible to return to the simplicity, individualism, and love of hard work that had initially created the American way of life.

This account of Grey's association with Arizona begins with an examination of his visits to the area. These visits are divided into four geographic areas: the Arizona Strip and the Grand Canyon, the northern Arizona Navajo and Hopi Indian reservations, the southern deserts of the Arizona–Sonora border, and the forests of the Mogollon Rim. Each region exhibited a peculiar natural environment and a unique history, and in each, human life developed and functioned in a manner adapted to the surroundings. Grey delighted in observing the effect of the environment on human life and on the forms that human society developed. The role of the frontier environment in determining the nature of human existence is the heart of Grey's portrait of the West. A review of the relevant literature, which echoes the four areas he visited, constitutes the second emphasis of this study. The novels, short stories, and articles he wrote about a particular region are addressed, and Grey's conception of life in that environment is discussed.

Grey portrayed each of the four regions of Arizona in a different way, focusing on the various types of people he encountered. Each of these four faces of Arizona represented a phase in the development of the American West. In the Arizona Strip and the Grand Canyon, he encountered Mormons, rustlers, horsetrackers, and cowboys. The northern Indian reservations taught him about the Navajo and Hopi Indians, government agents, traders, and missionaries. The southern deserts added Mexicans, soldiers, Yaqui Indians, prospectors, and ranchers. Homesteaders, cowboys, outlaws, sheep ranchers, and schoolteachers were found on the Mogollon Rim and in the Tonto Basin. These diverse types represented dramatically different lifestyles and societies.

Each locale also had unique environmental characteristics which set it apart from the other areas. The high deserts of the Arizona Strip, Grand Canyon, and northern reservations; the low deserts of the southern border; and the forested mountains of the Mogollon Rim each had its own particular landscape, challenges, and beauty. Grey found that these characteristics affected the residents, forming in them distinctive values and traits.

Films made from Grey's Arizona novels reflect another facet of Grey's conception of the West. Many of the early motion pictures were filmed where the action in the story was supposed to have occurred. Grey selected film locations himself in order to ensure authenticity, and he was often present during filming to give advice to the filmmakers. Later films, which were not always made on the exact location of the story and had a tendency to diverge from the plot as written by Grey, still retained the spirit of his novels and presented a picture of the West that was similar to what he had written. The transformation of his literature into the film medium allowed Grey's ideas to reach a much broader audience than was reached by the written word alone, and expressed his ideals of the West in a palatable, entertaining, and impressive format. The sixty-eight films made from his Arizona novels are discussed in the third portion of the study.

Through the motion picture medium, Grey utilized technological advances of the modern age to communicate his version of the West. In doing so, Grey himself became a pioneer; his works were used to develop the genre of the western film, and the extensive use of his stories as a source for movie plots makes him a giant among the popularizers of the western. Grey's stories, and stories that reflect the type of tales he produced, were later seen on television, a medium that was not developed until after his death. Zane Grey Theatre, which began in 1956, featured outdoor action and adventure stories, some of which came from Grey's books. No study of Grey's message, or of the effect of his message, would be complete without looking at these vehicles; those through which he reached his widest audience.

The Arizona Zane Grey described—gunmen, cowboys, the code of the West, stoic Indians, Mormons, villainous Mexicans, rustic home-steaders, and wholesome western girls—became his trademark, and were absorbed into the general conception of the West held by most Americans. Whatever else Zane Grey may have been, he was exciting. The portrait of Arizona and the West he bequeathed to many generations of Americans and to the world remains with us still.

ZANE GREY
IN ARIZONA

CHAPTER I

THE CANYON

O n Zane Grey's first visit to Arizona in 1906, he found a region in the turmoil of rapid change. Forty years had passed since the United States government created the territory of Arizona, and the area had made tremendous strides toward modernization and eventual statehood. The Apaches and Navajos were subdued and neatly stored on reservations, schools and churches were established, the trappings of law and order were apparent, and the Old West existed only in stories told by the oldtimers. Yet, the flavor of the Old West remained. Cowboys with jingling spurs ambled down the ranch-town streets, cattle round-ups took place every fall, Mormons and their many wives lived on their farms and ranches, and gunfights and saloon brawls occurred with shocking frequency. Mountain lions, bears, and wild mustangs roamed the northern mountains; prospectors, banditoes, and gila monsters roamed the southern deserts. Civilization ended at the town limits and the frontier took over from there. The luxuries of modern life and the primitive nature of the frontier mingled oddly in Grey's first impression of Arizona, but it was the frontier that captured his imagination. Grey became obsessed with the isolated, lonely land and he returned to Arizona more than twenty times.

Grey was thirty-three years old when he arrived in Arizona for the first time. His life had been pleasant and productive, but he was not content with its direction. He preferred fishing to pulling teeth, and was convinced that his true calling lay somewhere other than dentistry. He desired to become a writer. He had already written two novels, *Betty Zane* and *Spirit of the Border;* in progress was *The Last Trail*. All were based on family legends surrounding his great-grandfather, Ebenezer Zane, a Revolutionary War hero. Although these three novels were not commercially successful, Grey clung to his faith in his ability to become a successful author.

Supporting him in that faith was his wife, Lina. After an engagement of four years, throughout which Lina encouraged Grey's writing, the couple married in New York City in 1905. Lina, called Dolly by her friends and her husband, majored in English in college and was eager to use her skills. She frequently proofread and edited her fiancé's literary efforts, and was most likely the "wealthy patient" from whom he borrowed the money to publish his first novels. Although these did not sell well, and the dental practice was dwindling because of his habit of going fishing instead of going to work, "Doc" and Dolly decided to marry. At his fiancée's urging, the young Dr. Grey also decided to abandon his dental practice and become a full-time writer. The couple delayed their honeymoon, using money Dolly had recently inherited to purchase a small cottage in Lackawaxen, Pennsylvania; this base would serve as their home and an ideal setting for Grey to concentrate on his writing. In the early months of 1906, however, they treated themselves to an extensive tour of the West, traveling by rail to California.

One of the many stops the couple made on this excursion was a little railroad town in Arizona called Flagstaff, a stop on the Atchison, Topeka and Santa Fe line. After long days of traveling through arid desert, train travelers were delighted to feel the cool mountain air. In the shadows of the snowcapped San Francisco Peaks, Flagstaff was the cattle, timber, and railroad center of northern Arizona. It was also the gateway to the Grand Canyon, which, in 1906, was already a major attraction. Visitors stepped off the train and back in time in the frontier town. Most travelers checked into the Commercial Hotel, across the street from the train station, to spend a few days soaking in the sights and sounds of the West. Doc and Dolly spent four days in northern Arizona, even making the long and somewhat dangerous journey to the bottom of the Grand Canyon.[1]

This first encounter with Arizona was brief, but it made a lasting impression on Grey. The majestic mountains and the mysterious canyon introduced him to a world different from anything he had encountered in the East. Flagstaff was the doorway through which Grey entered this world. Arrival in the bustling little town preceded his adventures in other, more isolated regions. The organization and outfitting of his expeditions took place there, and Grey frequently spent a week or more exploring Flagstaff and meeting its people.

Grey's travels took him first to the Arizona Strip. Lying one hundred twenty miles north of Flagstaff on the far side of the Colorado River and the Grand Canyon, the strip was inaccessible to all but the most hardy traveler. Approaching the strip from the Arizona side, the wayfarer crossed the Painted Desert and the Kaibito Plateau before contending with the immense canyon and the Colorado River, an obstacle that could be crossed at only one point, Lee's Ferry. Crossing at the ferry could be accomplished only during times when the river was at its lowest point. The loss of horses, goods, and men during a crossing was not uncommon. Few travelers, therefore, were adventurous enough to hazard a trip to the Arizona Strip by way of Flagstaff and Lee's Ferry.

Deserts, canyons, and mountains separated the Arizona Strip from its neighboring lands to the north, east, and west. The traveler who approached it from the north journeyed across endless expanses of badlands, crossing the mountains of southwest Utah at Zion and, in the Dixie National Forest, the deep canyons of the Kolob Plateau or the high desert of the Kaiparowits Plateau. The route from Nevada in the west took the traveler across the treacherous, arid wastes of the Shivwits Plateau. Should entrance be attempted from the east, the traveler had to contend with the mighty Colorado River, which cuts a diagonal swath across Utah before entering the Grand Canyon in Arizona.

Because of its isolation, the Arizona Strip was a treasure trove of undisturbed wildlife and primeval forests, deserts, mountains, and canyons. From Buckskin Mountain to Kanab Canyon, the land presented magnificent feasts for the eye. Deer, mountain lions, and wild horses roamed the flatlands and the mountains; the mountain lions congregated in the rugged area just north of the canyon, called the Siwash. From the Kaibab Plateau on the southeastern part of the strip to Powell's Plateau farther west, the north rim of the Grand Canyon was mountainous and covered with cedar, open sage flats, and pine trees. Standing on the north rim, the visitor could see the San Francisco Peaks in the distance to the south, and the blood-colored Vermilion Cliffs of Utah to the north. At his feet yawned the frightening chasm of the canyon itself. Space for adventure, beauty, introspection, and ideas abounded in the isolated Arizona Strip.

Those most familiar with the strip were Mormons, members of the Church of Jesus Christ of Latter-Day Saints, whose isolated settlements were scattered through southern and western Utah and stretched exploring fingers onto the plateaus north of the canyon as well. The Mormons themselves originally regarded the strip as good for nothing more than a place to store Indians, although preliminary exploring and missionary parties, notably those led by Jacob Hamblin in the late 1850s and early 1860s, noted that there were a few places that might possibly be suitable for farming.[2] Throughout the 1870s and 1880s, Mormon settlement crept toward these desirable places in southern Utah and northern Arizona. The Mormons had a primary allegiance to their church, headquartered in Salt Lake City, Utah, and so the Arizona Strip, although geographically part of Arizona, was for all intents and purposes an appendage of Utah, imbued with Mormon culture and tradition.

Chief among the Mormons who resided in the Arizona Strip was Jim Emett, the patriarch who presided over the Colorado River crossing at Lee's Ferry. Mormons had operated this crossing since 1871, and Emett was sent to run it in 1896. Tall, with flowing grey hair, Emett resembled an Old Testament prophet.[3] There, beside the mighty Colorado, he created his own Garden of Eden. Emett, like many Mormons, practiced polygamy, and with his wives and children, planted and tilled, herded and hunted for his livelihood. Emett's cattle shared their plateau rangeland with a herd of buffalo belonging to another area resident, Charles Jesse "Buffalo" Jones.[4] Jones was a remnant of the late nineteenth-century frontier. An aging buffalo hunter, he had participated in the mass slaughter of the animals on the Great Plains in the 1870s. Then, after realizing the danger of extinction, he dedicated his life to the preservation of the lumbering animal. After gathering a herd from among the survivors, Jones drove them to Arizona in 1906, creating a buffalo preserve in the wild and lonely stretches of the Arizona Strip.

It was Jones's need for money for his preserve that drew Grey back to Arizona in 1907.[5] Jones consented to tour the major cities of the east coast, presenting a series of lectures about his buffalo preserve with the hope of inspiring his listeners, primarily eastern sportsmen, to contribute financial support. In addition to his descriptions of the preserve itself, the wild-looking Jones, dressed in buckskin, added color to his lectures by telling of life on the Arizona Strip, including his own remarkable feat of lassoing and capturing live, wild mountain lions. The eastern sportsmen were incredulous when they heard the old frontiersman's stories and, quite frankly, did not believe him. Grey was introduced to Jones by Alvah James, a South American explorer; he was fascinated by the tale and so intrigued with Jones's accounts of the Arizona Strip that he offered to travel to the buffalo preserve and record Jones's feat on film and paper.

Flagstaff was the meeting place for Jones and Grey in the spring of 1907, only fourteen months after Grey's first visit to Arizona and the Grand Canyon. From Flagstaff, Grey, with Buffalo Jones as his teacher and guide, would explore the land north of the canyon, land the tourist and the timid rarely saw. Plans were made for Grey, Jones, and a party of Mormon cowboys and wild horsetrackers to travel across the Painted Desert, cross the Colorado River at Lee's Ferry, move along the upper reaches of the Grand Canyon and, finally arrive at House Rock Valley, Jones's home. No trains existed to make this journey comfortable or easy; the entire route would be covered on horseback or on foot.

While the party made its preparations, Grey, the wide-eyed tenderfoot from the East, explored every corner of Flagstaff. His curiosity took him to a trial that had gained some notoriety. Jim Emett, the dignified Mormon who operated Lee's Ferry, had been accused of cattle theft by the Grand Canyon Cattle Company, a competitor whose cattle shared the rangeland of the Arizona Strip. Emett's serenity in the midst of adversity impressed Grey so much that when he was cleared of all charges, Grey invited him to join him and Jones on their journey to Lee's Ferry. Grey's admiration for Emett increased as Emett repeatedly proved his capability and his knowledge of desert lore on the long trek.[6]

The 1907 visit to Arizona introduced Grey to the first of four faces of the frontier that molded his western writing. Under the tutelage of Jones and Emett, Grey learned the art of survival. He experienced hunger, fear, loneliness, and danger, and he came to know men who faced these terrors every day of their lives. He learned to stay in the saddle all day long, sleep on the hard ground at night, and rise before daybreak to mount his horse once again.[7] He hunted, rode, and tracked mountain lions—he even shot one when it evaded Jones's lasso and leaped directly at him. Grey met Mormons, and while he admired many of their qualities, he disliked their practice of polygamy; he particularly pitied

Mormon women.[8] The life he found in the Arizona Strip was a life different from anything he had previously encountered in the East. Its values were simple, direct, and primitive; survival was the constant concern, and mistakes were deadly.

As they proceeded across the Painted Desert, Grey, Jones, and Emett approached the Grand Canyon, the Colorado River, and Emett's oasis. There they paused for a few days, resting men and animals in Emett's orchards and fields. After what seemed to be too brief a rest, the caravan departed again, crossing the Colorado and proceeding southwest forty miles toward the forests of Buckskin Mountain, House Rock Valley, and the buffalo preserve. Jones then escorted Grey into the forest, where they tracked mountain lions and captured one alive.[9]

The capture of the mountain lion was the high point of the entire trip. Grey's respect for Jones, the old frontiersman, increased tenfold when he saw him tirelessly pursuing that dangerous beast and following it into perilous places when other, younger, men abandoned the chase. Grey saw another side of Jones's nature, too. He observed how Jones drove men, horses, dogs, and mountain lions relentlessly and pitilessly, to the point of exhaustion and beyond, and referred to him as a "fiend."[10] Nevertheless, to Grey, Jones was the epitome of the frontiersman, exhibiting strengths and virtues of the frontier and the Old West in larger-than-life size.

Besides revealing Jones's qualities, the mountain lion hunt was memorable to Grey because of its setting. From the campsite on the north rim, the Grand Canyon assumed colors and moods that were not visible from the more accessible south rim, and these were continually changing. Grey arose before his companions in order to watch the sun illuminate the chasm, and he left camp at dusk to view it at its most mysterious, in the twilight. In years to come, Grey returned to the Grand Canyon many times, but was never able to define its attraction.[11]

The young author returned to his home and to his wife, but was a changed man. The northern deserts and mountains of Arizona awakened in him a hunger for the primitive life. In his writing, he tried to recapture the zest and excitement of his Arizona adventure, but this did not satisfy him for long. Within a year, he was back in Flagstaff preparing for another sojourn with Buffalo Jones on the north rim of the Grand Canyon.

This time Grey, Jones, David Dexter Rust (a Mormon explorer from southern Utah), Jim Owens (a ranger), and several others explored Powell's Plateau, an area within a bend of the Colorado River some distance west of House Rock Valley and Buckskin Forest.[12] In their explorations they stumbled upon Thunder River, a substantial stream composed almost altogether of falls and rapids that flowed through a luxuriant oasis called Surprise Valley. This pocket of beauty, surrounded by desert, captured the essence of the Arizona Strip for Grey: a place where life flourished and produced amazing loveliness despite the environment.

After exploring Surprise Valley, Jones and Grey traveled north to the small Arizona village of Fredonia and its neighbor in southern Utah, Kanab. Both were Mormon settlements, and Grey was able to observe Mormon life in a community setting rather than the isolated pockets he had previously encountered at Emett's oasis. Grey's interest in Mormonism was related to his feelings about Surprise Valley. He was intrigued by the struggle for survival in the high desert of the Arizona Strip, and searched for that startling flash of beauty that was sometimes found within that struggle. The Mormons were perfect human subjects for Grey's study: within a barren environment, they carved a unique society, one that differed from mainstream America. Their communities had elements of which Grey disapproved—namely polygamy—and the struggle to survive tended to inhibit compassion for others, yet Grey found a certain harmony in their desert existence. He explored their towns, met their people, and talked with them concerning their life, history, and feelings.

During this time, Grey conceived the idea of using the Mormon experience on the Arizona Strip as subject matter for his writing. Here were all the elements a writer needed: drama, passion, struggle, beauty, jealousy, repression, domination, romance, and the exotic.[13] Using the Arizona Strip as the setting, Grey decided to translate the Mormon experience into a western romance. Many of the Mormons he met became characters in the novel, while their society provided him with both plot and theme. He believed he was suited to interpret the Mormon way of life because of his firsthand knowledge of Mormon society, his acquaintance with many individual Mormons, his sympathy for their fight to exist, and even his disapproval of their practice of polygamy.[14] This mixture, in which sympathy and disapproval commingled, allowed him to be objective, he thought, in his estimation of their lives. Here, at last, Grey had found his literary opportunity. He returned to New York to begin writing. His efforts produced two romances set in the Arizona Strip, *Heritage of the Desert* (1910) and *Riders of the Purple Sage* (1912).

Fame came to him upon publication of these books, but was accompanied by loss. The wonder and beauty Grey found in the Arizona Strip primarily attracted him because the world had not yet discovered it. When he exposed the area to the world through his books, it became a familiar place, one still dear to him, but one with less power to excite. The author visited the Arizona Strip several more times, but never again embarked on the long, demanding treks of discovery that he had so enjoyed with Jones and Emett. In the spring of 1911, he briefly stopped at some of the sites of his earlier adventures.[15] In 1914, he returned once again, and occupied himself by climbing the San Francisco Peaks near Flagstaff and spending some time at the Grand Canyon.[16] In the summers of 1915 and 1916, he again briefly visited the Grand Canyon, staying at El Tovar, a hotel built by Fred Harvey on the south rim.[17] Much later, in 1924, he returned to the Arizona Strip in an attempt to save deer in danger of starvation on the north rim of the Grand Canyon.

In the past, the deer population had been controlled naturally by predatory mountain lions, but as more people moved to northern Arizona and established ranches and farms, a bounty was placed on the mountain lions to reduce their number and eliminate the threat to domestic animals. The bounty was effective; however, as the mountain lions disappeared, the deer population grew, and inevitably, exceeded its food supply. Residents of northern Arizona then became concerned about the situation and plans were made in the fall of 1924 to drive the deer down from their range, into the Grand Canyon, and then up again to the forest on the south rim.[18] Thirty to forty cowboys and rangers and about one hundred Navajo and Paiute Indians were hired. Grey heard of the plan and decided to take an active part in it.[19] He wanted to use the drive as an episode in a novel that was proposed for a movie, as well, and thought it would be exciting to capture the drive on film. He convinced Lasky Famous Players Corporation, of which he was a director, to finance the deer drive in return for exclusive motion picture rights. Grey claimed exclusive literary rights for himself.[20]

In December 1924, the Lasky film crew was on hand, and Grey and his entourage were on horseback, ready to aid in the drive. Unfortunately, no one had enlisted the cooperation of the deer. For three days, the animals were driven along the lower slopes of Buckskin Mountain toward Saddle Gap where they would be herded into the canyon. As the deer approached the gap, they broke and ran in all directions, and the great deer drive ended rather ignominiously.

Grey attributed the failure of the drive to inadequate preparation, lack of drivers, and the unexpected refusal of the deer to be driven.[21] More importantly, Grey saw in the deer drive the fate of the pristine land he so loved. Fifteen years before, he and Buffalo Jones had advised local government officials not to kill the mountain lions; their warnings were not heeded. The destruction of the balance of nature resulted in the plight of the starving deer and the necessity for a heroic attempt to save them.

Grey's books had helped publicize the area and drew people to the Arizona Strip, but the despoilation saddened him. He was a believer in the preservation of the nation's resources and opposed government or commercial measures that tampered with the natural course of the land and its wildlife. Three years before, in 1921, he had spoken out against the Colorado River Project, a plan to build dams along the river's course and use the water and hydroelectric power to support increased population. Grey believed that the project would ruin the river and deprive both Indians and animals of one of life's necessities.[22] Once again, he believed, conditions which led to the great Kaibab deer drive were a direct result of human interference with nature.

After this ill-fated but well-intentioned drive, Grey directed his attention to even more remote parts of Arizona, places that had not yet come to the attention of the rest of the world.

CHAPTER II

THE RESERVATION

Zane Grey needed the excitement of new discoveries to inspire his writing, and he recaptured this sense of adventure when he explored the second face of Arizona, the northern Indian reservations.

The Navajo Reservation sprawls across the high desert of northeastern Arizona and into Utah, New Mexico, and Colorado, while the Hopi Reservation occupies three Arizona mesas within the larger reservation. The Navajos' land, which encompasses over sixteen million acres, is a semi-arid region and is the traditional homeland of both the nomadic Navajo and the sedentary Hopi.

In the nineteenth century, however, the Navajo practice of raiding Hopi and neighboring Anglo settlements caused retaliatory measures to be taken against them. In 1863 and 1864, the United States Government moved the tribe to a reservation in eastern New Mexico called Bosque Redondo.[1] Four years later, after it became clear that this experiment had failed, the Navajos were allowed to return to their homeland. After this experience, they became peaceful shepherds and farmers, but continued to hold their neighbors, the Hopi, in scorn. Navajo success at raising sheep stimulated another controversy. Because more grazing land was required for their herds, the government increased the size of the

Navajo Reservation until it completely encircled the three Hopi Mesas, home of their traditional enemies.

On this huge expanse of desert, the Navajo continued to live much as their ancestors had, performing religious rituals, herding sheep, tending crops, and teaching children the ancient ways.[2] Harbingers of Anglo culture entered this placid existence in the form of missionaries, traders, and agents. These people brought with them the trappings of an alien civilization that had values, rules, and religions that differed drastically from those of the Navajo as well as the Hopi.[3]

As Navajo and Hopi encountered this foreign society, their ancient ways of life underwent rapid change. The old was challenged by the new, and the Indians faced the task of adapting themselves and their society to a strange new world. Adding to the problem, Anglo society was not always represented on the Indian reservations by the most honorable of men. The Navajo and Hopi all too often were the victims of greedy and corrupt traders, agents, and missionaries, although there were many others who were honest and compassionate. Despite the influence of the United States government, few Anglos were to be found on the reservations and little was known about them or those who lived on them by most easterners when Grey first visited the area in 1911.

Though they led him to new adventures—particularly on the Navajo Reservation—Grey's initial excursions were partially the result of complications that changed his original plan to return to the Arizona Strip.[4] Buffalo Jones, away on his own African tour, was not available to accompany him.[5] Jim Emett was also unavailable, so Grey made arrangements for David Dexter Rust, who had accompanied him and Jones in 1907 and 1908, to act as his guide.[6] Grey and Rust planned to meet in Flagstaff in April, then travel north, but Rust was unable to reach Flagstaff, as the crossing at Lee's Ferry was too dangerous due to early spring flooding of the Colorado. In Rust's place, Grey hired a Flagstaff man, Al Doyle, as guide, and planned to spend several weeks touring a part of Arizona he had not previously experienced before traveling to the Arizona Strip.[7]

Grey could have found no one better qualified to lead him to new places than Al Doyle. Doyle, like Buffalo Jones, was a remnant of the Old West of the 1870s and 1880s, and had participated in many different phases of frontier life. He was a member of one of the rail gangs that laid the final railroad track joining the Union Pacific with the Central Pacific, creating the nation's first transcontinental railroad. He was present when the gold, silver, and lead spikes were driven to commemorate that event. Doyle had been a buffalo hunter, a miner, a freighter, a cowboy, and a rancher; after he sold his cattle ranch in northern Arizona, he retired to Flagstaff where he and his son, Lee, accepted occasional commissions to guide visitors through the West. Besides knowing the places in Arizona that appealed to Grey's taste for the wilderness, Doyle's tales of life in the frontier West were rich material for Grey's writing.[8]

Al Doyle introduced Grey to the world of the Indian reservations in northern Arizona, and to the people who lived there, and Grey discovered another unique way of life upon the high desert. The world of hogan and pueblo, the stoic Indian, isolation, the flash of brilliant color in a Navajo blanket, and vivid hues of the desert in which the Indian made his home set fire to Grey's imagination, and he was eager to capture it on paper. Here was a new inspiration, another unexplored world.

Doyle took Grey across Marsh Pass in northeastern Arizona, then further east to Kayenta, a trading post located on the Navajo Reservation and operated by John and Louisa Wetherill, who had begun trading with the Navajos in 1906. The Wetherills were representative of the best that the Anglo world offered the Indian. They were honest, hard-working, and deeply concerned about the welfare and just treatment of the Navajo and Hopi. Louisa studied Navajo language and culture, and John Wetherill traveled extensively within the reservation and knew more about its terrain and its natural wonders than most Anglos in the vicinity.[9] The Wetherills were regarded as friends by both Navajos and Hopis, an accomplishment that required great diplomatic skill. Grey spent several days at Kayenta and came to know the couple; from them, the author began to learn something of life on the reservation, and his curiosity was aroused.

During his stay at Kayenta, Grey was entertained by Louisa Wetherill's accounts of Navajo stories and legends.[10] Most of the legends were connected with natural landmarks and explained how those sites came to be and their relationship to the Navajo people. Several of the legends mentioned *Nonnezoshe,* a giant natural arch in the northern part of the Navajo Reservation close to the Colorado River and the Utah border, but east of the Grand Canyon and the Arizona Strip.[11] The Navajos regarded this stone edifice as their supreme deity. Grey developed an all-consuming desire to visit *Nonnezoshe,* which he named Rainbow Bridge, and asked John Wetherill to take him there.

Wetherill had earlier been a part of the original Anglo expedition, led by Dr. Byron Cummings, a professor from the University of Utah. The group was actually guided to the bridge, however, by a Paiute Indian, Nasja Begay, and reached the site in 1909, only two years before Grey's visit to Kayenta.[12] The route to the bridge was long and arduous; few dared attempt it. There were no roads—only paths and trails marked the way to the landmark. The entire trip had to be made on horseback or foot, and Wetherill was reluctant to embark on such a journey with a tenderfoot easterner in tow, despite the fact that this particular tenderfoot had already spent some time in the Arizona wilderness with no less a frontiersman than Buffalo Jones. As a result, Grey was unsuccessful in his attempt to induce Wetherill to take him to the bridge on that first visit.

Undaunted, Grey visited Kayenta twice more, each time in the company of Al Doyle, before he convinced Wetherill to escort him to *Nonnezoshe*. Finally, in the spring of 1913, the trader consented to lead Grey and his friends on an excursion to this sacred Navajo monument. Wetherill's reluctance grew when Grey appeared at Kayenta that spring accompanied by an entourage that included two women, all wanting to go to *Nonnezoshe*.[13]

The women, Elma Swartz and Lillian Wilhelm, were part of the life Grey adopted following his success as a writer, and they revealed a different aspect of his personality. Lillian Wilhelm, a member of the intellectual set of New York City and Dolly's cousin, was an artist interested in illustrating romances written by this popular new author.[14] Although Grey's novels sold well and gained favorable reviews during these early years, the literary elite did not accept him as one of them. Grey, ever attempting to conquer new worlds, was determined to win their acceptance and admiration. Lillian Wilhelm's presence on this excursion to the land of Grey's inspiration was intended to win for him the favor of the eastern literary crowd.

There was also a sensual side to Grey, apparent in his love of beautiful women. He was responsive to color, shape, texture, and beauty; this receptiveness allowed him to create the intricate descriptions that were so widely acclaimed by reviewers and that form such a large part of his work's appeal. In his younger days, this sensuality was submerged in his writing and focused upon the new land he discovered in Arizona. Once he conquered the land and captured its essence on paper for the world to enjoy, he was in need of new outlets for this facet of his artistry. He found that in surrounding himself with lovely young women he satisfied his own need for beauty and quickened his sense of adventure.

Women accompanied Grey on his western trips as early as 1913. They added to the confusion and chaos that surrounded the Grey party as it prepared for sojourns in the wilderness, but they also added to the color and intrigue that surrounded Grey's arrival in small western towns. Emotions ran high during these expeditions, sometimes resulting in arguments. Referring to his brother as "Doc," as did most of his family and friends, Romer Grey once disgustedly wrote to his sister-in-law, Dolly,

> Doc and Elma have been fighting for two days, but Doc smiles tonight so maybe they have things fixed-up by now. I am commencing to believe there is very little hope of ever getting any harmony out of this kind of existence.[15]

Frequently the women were left behind in camp while the men hunted, fished, and escaped from the "feminine element."[16] These extended trips with close male companions and beautiful young women provided Grey with adventure, excitement, and intrigue.

Grey's craving for female companionship was not, however, an obsession for him. Indeed, it represented only a portion of his life. Another side of Grey valued the old-fashioned virtues of home, family, and fidelity. This is the side of Grey seen by the public through his novels, and represented in his private life by his wife, Dolly, and his three children, Romer, Betty, and Loren. Dolly waited for him to come home from his ramblings, once writing,

> The kiddies and I are still here for you to come back to. Maybe someday you'll come home to stay—and we'll have a *real* home of our own. But don't wait too long, dear. Even inborn instincts become atrophied from disuse.[17]

Though he roamed in far-away lands and with rivals for his affection, Dolly stood steadfastly by, always encouraging him.

While waiting for her husband to return, Dolly assumed responsibility for handling the business side of Grey's success. She received requests and negotiated agreements with publishers, magazines, and motion picture studios. She disbursed and invested the money received from the sales of Grey's writing, and handled the family's badly muddled tax situation. Dolly was usually successful in her business ventures, and the huge fortune Grey accumulated during the 1920s was in part attributable to her astute handling of financial matters. That the family fortune survived the Great Depression of the 1930s was also due to her financial acumen. Grey himself abhorred the details of business, and time and again proved that he had no talent in that direction. Agents, friends, and his wife begged him to keep his hands off of the business side of his career, and, for the most part, he was only too glad to turn it over to Dolly and then wander off on another of his long trips.[18]

Despite Dolly's adept handling of the details of fame, success began to pall for Grey. When he arrived at Kayenta in the spring of 1913 with two women in tow, he was ready for new adventures. A journey to the great monument of the Navajo was very attractive.

Wetherill arranged for Nasja Begay to guide the party, which consisted of the trader, Grey, Al Doyle, Lillian Wilhelm, Elma Swartz, and a cook, George Morgan.[19] The entire group, plus a supply wagon, left Kayenta and traveled west to Navajo Mountain. There they left the wagon, the cook, and the ladies and proceeded by horseback. They traveled around the base of Navajo Mountain and then northwest to *Nonnezoshe*. The first portion of the trail took them through Monument Valley, land of towering buttes and strange landforms.

Nonnezoshe, like the Grand Canyon, overwhelmed Grey. He saw more in it than its mere physical presence; he sensed that the changeless natural bridge had a message for him, which he in turn would give to his readers. The idea for a story took root. It would be based upon the Indians' struggle to retain their culture and, at the same time, accommodate newcomers to their land. It would also incorporate the message for humanity found in *Nonnezoshe* and be set in the timeless beauty of Monument Valley. While Grey found the stimulation he needed for his work on the remote Indian reservation of northern Arizona, it was the Navajo's natural bridge that spoke to him of the drama of the Indians' life.

Having spent several days at the arch, Wetherill and Nasja Begay led Grey and his friends back by a different route, following Navajo Trail south to Marsh Pass, where Morgan and the wagon waited for them. On the way, Grey observed an ancient Indian custom.[20] Lying beside the trail was a huge boulder, which appeared to weigh over two hundred pounds and was worn smooth, apparently from handling. Nasja Begay explained that each Indian boy, as he approached manhood, tested his

strength by trying to move the stone away from the mountain. During
the forty or fifty years prior, according to Begay, the boulder was moved
only two miles. In fact, the lengthiest move had been made just a few
years before, when the rock had been moved over fifty feet. This
glimpse into Indian values intrigued the writer so that he used the custom in several of his stories that utilized reservation settings.[21]

Life on the Indian reservations of northern Arizona revealed a different type of primitive existence to Grey. People who lived there were en-
meshed in the same elemental struggle for survival as those who lived on
the Arizona Strip. Yet reservation dwellers faced the additional challenge of an alien culture that exploited them and then threatened to rob
them of their own culture, uniqueness, and pride. This struggle, set as it
was in the desolate beauty of the high northern deserts, provided the
theme for Grey's literary version of his impressions of the second face of
Arizona and the West. His purpose was to tell the rest of the world the
Indians' story and to paint a picture of their harmonious existence,
threatened by the strident notes of encroaching Anglo civilization. He
wanted to tell, too, of the representatives of Anglo culture, both those
who greedily exploited the Indians' plight for personal gain and those
who fought for justice for the Indian. The weaving of this difficult tale
occupied him from 1913, when he was so greatly impressed by *Nonnezoshe*, to 1922, when he completed his narrative on this region.

Grey made another visit to the Navajo Reservation in the summer of
1914.[22] On this visit, he entered from Gallup, New Mexico, then proceeded overland to Flagstaff, visiting and fishing in Oak Creek Canyon
while in the region. He climbed the San Francisco Peaks, then traveled
across the desert into southern Utah, returning through Monument Valley, Kayenta, Marsh Pass, and Tuba City. After visiting Grand Canyon
again, he departed from Arizona and traveled to California. Although an
extensive visit in terms of time involved and area covered, it did not take
him into any new territory representing new worlds to conquer.

When Grey finished a novel set in the reservation, he visited Navajo-
land again to verify locations and to reaffirm his initial impressions. He
brought with him this time an Arizona artist, Mrs. Westbrook Robertson.[23] She was to illustrate his reservation novel, and wanted to view the
actual story location before she began. This was not an excursion of discovery, but a business trip. The reservation no longer held the same fascination for Grey. He had unlocked its secrets, explored its meaning,
and reproduced his image of it in writing. Its exposure to the world,

much of which came through his writing, reduced its charm for him.

Grey visited the reservation once again in 1923, to show its natural beauty to the film industry.[24] He came to Arizona to assist with the Flagstaff-area filming of one of his novels but took advantage of the situation to introduce the well-known director, Jesse Lasky, to the reservation's potential as a location. Grey thought the natural setting of the reservation to be ideal for the filming of his Indian novels, and other stories as well. He escorted Lasky to several northeastern Arizona sites, pointing out the photogenic qualities of each. Among the spots were Keams Canyon and Rainbow Bridge.

Many changes had taken place on the Navajo Reservation since Grey first visited it in 1911. In 1923, Grey's party traveled to the different locations by automobile over dirt roads, rather than on horseback over rough trails as Grey, Doyle, and Wetherill had. Because the greater accessibility of remote reservation areas attracted increasing numbers of tourists, it was becoming commercialized and was beginning to cater to tourists' demands and expectations. Much of the interest was generated by Grey's novels and the films made from them, and he was pleased by their success; yet he saw that the ancient way of life was disappearing, and that the change was accelerated by these new pressures.

After 1923, Grey did not visit the reservation again. He had extracted all that he could from it, exhausting its attraction for him. The reservation was no longer the undisturbed pocket of primitivism it had been in 1911. Lamenting the disruption of the Indians' solitude, he turned his attention to the desolation of the southern Arizona deserts.

CHAPTER III

THE DESERT

The deserts of southern Arizona stretch across the south-central and southwestern corner of the state and down into northern Mexico, and bear little resemblance to those of the high plateaus to the north. Hot and dry, most of the land is below three thousand feet in elevation, although there are isolated places in Arizona's southeastern corner that are a few thousand feet higher. The southwestern corner receives only three to four inches of rain annually, while the southeastern portion receives only slightly more. Cactus, yucca, creosote, and mesquite dot the barren landscape. This climate is harsh on humans, animals, and plants, and its lack of water discourages all but the most adaptable.

This land differed from anything Grey had yet explored, and was also unique in that it retained a strong Spanish flavor. First under Spanish control, then a part of Mexico (1821–1854), this desolate strip of land—which extended into modern-day New Mexico—was acquired by the United States in 1854 through the Gadsden Purchase. Within Arizona, the area south of Tucson along the Santa Cruz River was settled primarily by Spanish colonists.

They left their mark on the entire region: names of towns, rivers, and mountains are Spanish, and the most common architectural style—with

whitewashed adobe walls decorated with strings of chili peppers drying
in the sun—is characteristic of Mexico. Spanish culture remains vital
and dynamic by continual contact with the border communities of northern Mexico.[1]

Also because of the area's proximity to Mexico, events in that country tend to boil over into southern Arizona. Even in Zane Grey's time,
news of the United States' nearest southern neighbor was of great interest to American readers and frequently made the headlines in the United
States newspapers. Mexico had a fairly stable, though corrupt, government led by President Porfirio Diaz from 1876 to 1911.[2] In 1910, dis-
content with the Diaz dictatorship initiated a revolution, and violent re-
bellion arose all over Mexico, but most of it took place in the northern
provinces, close to Arizona. Revolutionary leader Francisco Madero
crossed the border into the United States several times and frequently
directed the uprising from U.S. vantage points, while his supporters—
Pascual Orozco, Pancho Villa, and Emiliano Zapata—conducted ma-
neuvers very close to the border. Skirmishes took place in the twin
towns of Naco, Arizona and Naco, Sonora (Mexico); fifty-four noncom-
batant Americans were killed or wounded in these battles.[3] In an attempt
to confine the revolutionary activity to Mexico, the United States government stationed twenty thousand troops along the border, and Madero
was forced to join the guerrillas in northern Chihuahua. By 1911, the
revolutionaries were victorious and placed Madero in office as President
of Mexico.

Madero's success was shortlived; by February of 1912, when Grey
made his initial visit to southern Arizona, the borderlands were again
aflame with revolutionary activity. When Madero, as president, failed to
institute promised reforms, Pascual Orozco declared him a traitor and
led an armed uprising against him. Orozco was defeated by Mexican
federal troops under the command of General Victoriano Huerta, and
fled across the border into Arizona. It was not as easy to cross the border
in 1912 as it had been just the year before. The United States government increased border protection by the addition of eighty thousand
troops; one hundred thousand men patrolled the boundary between
Mexico and the United States. Opportunities for confrontations between
Mexican federal troops, revolutionary guerrillas, and United States soldiers increased. Furthermore, a clash between Mexican fighters and
United State troops carried more serious consequences than before, as
Arizona was granted statehood on February 14, 1912. National pride in-

sisted on intervention and retaliation, should Mexican troops invade an American state and engage in battle on American soil.

Grey arrived in southern Arizona during this tense situation. His visit was suggested by a close friend, Robert Hobart Davis, a New York City journalist.[4] Davis saw the setting for a novel of western romance in the revolutionary cauldron of Mexico and southern Arizona. Upon arriving in this hotbed of revolutionary activity, Grey concurred with Davis's suggestion; possibilities for intrigue, danger, and romance sparked his imagination. The result was *Desert Gold,* a novel set in southern Arizona in which the activities of federal Mexican troops, insurgents, and Arizona ranchers caught in the cross-currents of the revolution were interwoven.

Grey was intrigued by the plight of these borderland Americans. They suffered numerous depredations at the hands of soldiers, regardless of which country or faction they represented. Many of the revolutionary guerrillas resorted to theft when their own supplies ran low, and American ranches were their source of food and livestock. Bands of Mexican guerrillas would also harass the border settlements for no other purpose than terrorism. Although Grey admired the pure-blooded, aristocratic Spanish, he developed hatred, contempt, and distrust of Mexicans, regardless of their political affiliation, as a result of the outrages against ranchers caught in the path of the revolution.[5]

The Mexican government's policy toward the Yaqui Indians also intensified Grey's antagonism toward Mexicans.[6] The Yaqui Indians of Sonora resisted a Mexican attempt to deprive them of their land in the 1880s; the Mexicans wanted to replace them with Creoles, imported to establish cotton and rice plantations.[7] The Yaquis retreated to the mountains and resisted every armed force sent against them. Starvation finally forced them out of their strongholds, and they were sold into slavery by the Mexican government and transported to the Yucatán Peninsula to labor on the hemp plantations. Overwork, disease, and harsh treatment decimated their numbers. The enslavement ended in 1910 and the survivors returned to Sonora where they found the Creoles farming their land. The spectacle of the once-proud Yaquis, now defeated and discouraged, inflamed Grey's hatred of the Mexicans, and he idealized their pride and dignity in short stories such as "Yaqui."

The desert itself also attracted Grey. It afforded him another chance to investigate the ways in which the environment influenced its inhabitants.[8] This southern Arizona desert provided far fewer of the necessities for survival to its inhabitants than did the Arizona Strip or the northern reservations. At the same time, it had a direct and vicious effect on the life—human, animal, or plant—that was there. Survival was accomplished by only the most hardy, tough, and obstinate. Anything that remained in the desert for any length of time was altered. Grey believed that the desert encouraged people to regress to the primitive, and that it intensified character traits, be they evil or good. He also believed it taught the weak to be strong, but encouraged the strong to admit defeat. For Grey, the desert was a crucible in which human souls were melted and transformed, their final shapes determined by their internal elements, stripped of the tawdry plating of civilization.

Grey's fascination with the danger and romance of revolution, his contempt for Mexicans and sympathy for American bystanders, his admiration of the Yaquis, and, above all, his obsession with the desert were developed thematically in his work. His spring 1912 visit to the region showed him these diverse motifs and gave him the opportunity to explore the area and develop his literary conception. Grey found that his initial impressions were the strongest and most vital; they provided him with the material from which he could develop plot and theme. Just as he did not return to the reservation until his writing was complete, Grey did not visit the southern frontier again until he finished two novels, *Desert Gold* and *The Light of the Western Stars,* both of which developed the themes of revolution and the desert.

It was the filming of these two novels that called him once again to the southern frontier in 1919, where he found that much had changed.[9] The border was no longer aflame with revolution; tourists and the trappings of civilization were filtering into the area, and the wild southern deserts were becoming staid and respectable. Once again, the land no longer possessed him; while he continued to visit the southern deserts occasionally throughout the 1920s, the trips were simply vacations. His creative passion for the land was exhausted with the writing of his novels. The Mogollon Rim now claimed his attention.

CHAPTER IV

THE FOREST

The Mogollon Rim country of east-central Arizona offered beautiful mountain scenery, and a bloody history from which Grey could draw both story lines and characters. The southern edge of the Colorado Plateau, this rugged rock escarpment drops fifteen hundred feet into a basin immediately to the south and divides Arizona's high land from the desert that surrounds Phoenix and Tucson, more than a hundred miles to the south. Tall ponderosa pine, Utah juniper, piñon pine, quaking aspen, oak, fir, and spruce trees flourish at the 8,000' elevation, and make the rim country cool and deliciously shady in the summer, gloriously colorful in the fall. Mountain lion, black bear, mule deer, wild turkey, squirrel, chipmunk, and beaver provided food for the settler and sport for the hunter. Many mountain streams, particularly Tonto Creek, are rich with trout, and the area abounds with wild flowers of every hue from April to October. The summer months are temperate, with the mercury rarely climbing much above eighty. Winter temperatures plunge well below freezing and snow blankets the ground from mid-October to mid-March. Compared to the areas Grey had previously explored, the Mogollon Rim was an abundant Eden in the wilderness, offering its charms to all who sought them.

Agents of the Spanish New World empire were the first Europeans on the rim. Juan Vasquez de Coronado and his army of explorers marched into the rim country in 1540 on their way to the legendary Seven Cities of Cibola.[1] Because Coronado was more interested in gold than in forests and streams, the area's natural beauty did not detain him long. The brief Spanish visits had little, if any, impact on the region. Later, the rim's tranquility was shattered by more intrusive visitors.

The Tonto Apaches, a subtribe of the Western Apaches, called the rim country home as early as 1650[2]; though they lived in harmony with their environment, they were not always harmonious neighbors. The Apaches, understandably reluctant to give up their land to increasing numbers of Anglos who flooded the West after the Civil War, resisted encroachment. The Apache Wars raged across central and southern Arizona, with some of the bloodiest episodes taking place in the idyllic setting of the Mogollon Rim.[3] The peaceful countryside was torn by the Battle of Skull Cave (1872) and the Battle of Turret Butte (1873); both pitted General George Crook and his troops against hostile Apaches. The battles of Cibecue and Fort Apache (1881) again splintered the silence of the rim. The final confrontation between the Apaches and the United States Army in Arizona occurred in 1882, atop what is now called Battleground Ridge. The Battle of Big Dry Wash resulted in the deaths of twenty-two Apaches and the flight of the rest after only four hours of fighting. When the dust settled, the Apaches had been subdued and the way was finally cleared for pioneers, ranchers, and homesteaders to settle the rim country.

They came to Arizona from every part of the nation. The Haught family of Texas was typical of those who settled in the area. A. L. "Babe" Haught and his brother, John, left their home in Dallas, Texas, in 1897 and took the train to Globe, Arizona.[4] There, the two men were befriended by local citizens, who answered their questions about good areas to homestead by recommending the sparsely populated area along Tonto Creek. Despite warnings of hostile Indians, bears, and mountain lions, the brothers departed on foot for the Tonto Basin, just below the Mogollon Rim. After eight days of walking, they arrived at the rim and chose sites to homestead; they kept busy during the next year by constructing cabins, plowing and planting fields, and hunting. The two men were joined in the spring of 1898 by Babe's wife, Ella, their baby son, Eddie Rowe, and John's wife, Mary and their two children, four-year-old Lee and two-year-old Verdie. It was not long before Babe's family included two more sons as well as three daughters.

The Haughts formed the nucleus of the small Tonto Basin community. Babe made a living by hunting mountain lion and bear for bounty
money, driving a freight wagon between Payson and Flagstaff, working
on Roosevelt Dam in 1902, and acting as a hunting guide; in addition,
he raised crops, pigs, and chickens.[5] Henry Haught, a cousin, and Pink
Haught, Babe's brother, also homesteaded in the rim country. As time
went on and the Tonto Basin became more heavily populated, the
Haughts retained a special prominence as one of the earliest pioneer
families.

The event that drew Zane Grey, however, took place in 1887, ten
years before the Haughts' arrival. The Pleasant Valley War was one of
the most violent and bloody feuds of the frontier; the main participants
were the Tewksbury family and the Graham family. Responsibility for
the conflict is unclear—according to some, it began when the Tewksburys, who herded sheep for the Daggs brothers of Flagstaff, moved
their herds south of the rim into the Tonto Basin where the Grahams
ranged their cattle.[6] Others state that there were Tewksburys who
worked for the Grahams and protested the Grahams' practice of rustling
cattle from Mormons who settled in the vicinity of the rim as well as
from residents of Pleasant Valley to the northeast.[7] Still others assert that
the Grahams and Tewksburys differed over the division of cattle they
both stole from Jim Stinson, although the action that precipitated the
violence was the movement of Daggs brothers' sheep onto the Graham
cattle range by the Tewksburys.[8]

The most detailed and accurate account indicates that the catalyst for
the feud was the Graham family's cattle rustling activities, compounded
by the presence of a group of cowboys from the Hashknife outfit who
had been chased out of the Holbrook area.[9] While there was an incident
involving sheep, the heart of the feud was the rivalry between rustlers
and ranchers, rather than sheep ranchers versus cattle ranchers.

Whatever the cause, violence erupted and governed the rim country
for five years. When it ended, the fatalities totaled twelve Grahams and
three Tewksburys; every male Graham was killed, only one Tewksbury
survived, and he was understandably reluctant to talk.[10] For years afterward, the residents of the rim refused to discuss the feud with outsiders.
The Pleasant Valley War left scars, and only the most persistent and
dedicated investigator could uncover information, and then only after
acceptance by the community and proof of absolute trustworthiness.

Grey heard about the Pleasant Valley War from Harry Adams, a New Mexican rancher who once lived in the Tonto Basin. The story intrigued him, so he asked Al Doyle, whom he knew had been in northern Arizona at the time of the feud, for more information. Doyle's version differed markedly from Adams's, however. This discrepancy provoked the writer's curiosity and he decided to further research the matter as background for a novel.[11]

Doyle took Grey and his brother, Romer (R. C.), along with Elma Swartz and a companion, to the Mogollon Rim in the fall of 1918.[12] Ostensibly, the purpose of the trip was to hunt bear, mountain lion, and wild turkey in the White Mountains, but Grey was far more interested in uncovering the real story behind the Pleasant Valley War. To guide them on their hunting and exploring trip, Grey and Doyle hired Babe Haught and his three grown sons. Two months were spent hunting and tramping through the rim's wilderness. Grey discovered an area of Arizona that was unsurpassed for its sheer, green, rugged loveliness, but at the end of his time there, was no nearer to finding the truth than he had been at the beginning of his trip. Undaunted, he planned to return the next year and try again.

In the autumn of 1919, Grey went back to the Tonto Basin. This time, the hunting party was made up of Grey and R. C., R. C.'s wife, Al Doyle and his son Lee, Elma Swartz and her friend, the Haughts, and Ben Copple, an old-timer in the Tonto Basin. Grey and his brother each got a bear, the former's weighing over eight hundred pounds. More importantly, Grey felt he was successful in his search for the real story of the Pleasant Valley War. He met an elderly man, Elan Boles, who told the novelist his version of the feud.[13] Boles, a longtime area resident, had lived through the feud and his account endorsed the rustlers-versus-honest ranchers theme. Convinced that he possessed the truth, Grey returned to his home, now located in southern California, and commenced writing.

When he visited the rim once again the following fall, he was in for a surprise. Everybody wanted to tell him their version of the feud, and no two accounts agreed. He was deluged with a mass of information, which left him more confused than ever about the Pleasant Valley War. Despite many valiant efforts, Grey never did learn the truth of the matter. This was no deliberate attempt to deceive him; rather, it reflected the reality that an accurate account of the origins of the Graham-Tewksbury feud was buried under the debris of emotions, opinions, and loyalties accumulated during the feud itself and in the thirty years that had passed. The people themselves did not know what started the war, nor did they understand why it had happened.[14]

Although he did not find out what provoked the feud, Grey did learn something else of great value: he loved the Mogollon Rim country, which he renamed the Tonto Rim because it was easier to pronounce. It was rich with material for his writing. The setting, the people, the difficulties encountered as homes were built, triumphs celebrated, rustic joys, and devastating sorrows all formed a colorful backdrop for his western romances. Here was the quiet and serenity he needed to create his novels. Here, too, was material for characters, setting, plot, and theme. Should the work grow tiresome, he could indulge in his favorite pastimes of hunting and fishing. In short, the rim country offered everything for which he could ask. He decided to build a hideaway there, a retreat from the world, where he could find inspiration for his novels.

Three acres of land on the Haught ranch provided the location for the hideaway. Grey purchased the site in the fall of 1920, commissioned the Haughts to construct the building, and left for the east coast. He had in mind a rough-hewn log cabin, similar to the Haught's house, but he forgot to tell his construction crew what he wanted. The Haughts packed in Arizona timber, milled in Winslow, and built a house they thought would be appropriate for a famous writer from the East. When Grey returned in 1921, he expected to find a rustic cabin in the woods; instead, he found a city bungalow, complete with white paint and green trim.[15]

Any disappointment felt in the lodge itself was quickly dispelled by Grey's pleasure in its setting. The cabin was tucked away just underneath the rim and there was a magnificent view on all sides. To the north, in back of the cabin, the pine-covered escarpment towered. To the south, a panorama of forests stretched to distant blue mountains. In the east was the Tonto Basin and Pleasant Valley. A wide veranda encircled the building, allowing Grey and his guests to enjoy every aspect of the scenery.

The cabin itself was strictly a hunting lodge. It consisted of one large central room and a small lean-to kitchen in the back. There was also an attic, used as a storage room or as a place to dry hides. There were no bedrooms; Grey and his guests slept outside in tents or on the ground under the Arizona stars.[16]

Grey's delight in his cabin was dimmed by the illness of his longtime friend, Al Doyle. The old guide, who had accompanied him on many visits to Arizona and had shown him the state's treasures, was dying of cancer. Grey stopped in Flagstaff and spent several hours at his friend's bedside, reminiscing with him about their times together. He cherished the hours spent with his friend even more when Al died, only one week later.[17]

Doyle's death symbolized the end of an era to Grey. The plainsmen, cowboys, and pioneers neared the end of their time, and with their passing, the frontier of the Old West itself disappeared. The West had become a different place. No longer a rugged and lonely wilderness, it was tame, civilized, and respectable. Grey loved the simplicity of the Old West, and idealized its values of independence, honesty, strength, work, and courage. He could not help but wonder if the modern age had comparable values to replace those of the frontier. Gloomily, he predicted it did not.[18]

Al's son, Lee, was typical of the second generation of westerners. In many ways he was a frontiersman like his father; he was a cowboy, a woodsman, and a rancher. He knew horses better than he knew people, and had more admiration and respect for them as well. His face was bronzed from constant exposure to the elements, and he was accustomed to loneliness. He could find his way across uncharted forest and desert, yet the city and its crowds puzzled him. Lee Doyle avoided the sophistication of the city, preferring to be alone with his horse and perhaps one or two close companions.

There was no place for a man of these qualities in the modern world of the 1920s. The frontier days were gone, and even Arizona was becoming comparatively crowded. Roads invaded the heart of the wilderness, and carloads of tourists ogled the scenery while smoking cigarettes and sipping beer. Needing to make a living, Lee Doyle put himself at the tourists' disposal as guide, companion, and professional hunter. Although he despised the commercialization of the wilderness, he made local arrangements for movie companies who wished to film on location in Arizona, and eventually became the owner of a four-legged movie star, Rex, "King of Wild Horses."[19] Thus, this man of the frontier, fitted more for the West of a century before, paradoxically found his niche in the modern world as an employee of those who destroyed the wilderness by their presence.

Grey saw the value in this man; he, too, used Doyle's expertise at hunting and tracking and his knowledge of frontier life and conditions. Lee Doyle became Grey's agent in Arizona, handling matters concerning supplies, horses, and hired hands for Grey's trips to Arizona. As important, he became Grey's friend and teacher.

Although Grey saw the gradual demise of the Old West and regretted its passing, as did Lee Doyle, he continued to visit, research its history, enjoy its physical beauty, and learn to know its people. He spent several months at the Tonto Basin cabin in the fall of 1922, accompanied by his brother and several friends from California.[20] The Haughts and Lee Doyle joined him at the cabin, and they had an exciting time hunting bear, fishing, and basking in the magnificent scenery and atmosphere of the rim.

When Grey arrived in Arizona in the fall of 1923 for another stay, he had several tasks to accomplish in addition to his annual bear hunt. One of his novels was being filmed on location in Flagstaff and Oak Creek Canyon and he wanted to observe its progress. Also, he wished to show Jesse Lasky, director of the movie company, other possible filming locations. Grey was eager for the people of Arizona to grow and profit from the movie companies' interest in the area and from the increased tourism this would bring; he publicly encouraged the town of Flagstaff to build hotels and to welcome increased prosperity.[21]

In 1926, Grey brought his oldest son, Romer, and his daughter, Betty Zane, to the cabin, where he and his children spent the better part of two months hunting with Lee Doyle in the Arizona forests; Grey and his son each got a bear, making the adventure a success. Although Romer had visited Arizona in 1918, this was Betty's first trip to the state. Grey took his family through the bustling metropolis of Phoenix and north through Salt River Canyon, avoiding the route through Flagstaff because the road was not in good repair. Too, facilities in Flagstaff were often crude, he felt, sufficient for a man who planned to "rough it" for a few months in the wilderness but inappropriate for a family vacation. Phoenix, of course, had all the latest accommodations.

Passing through the city on the way to his cabin, Grey returned to Flagstaff in 1927, his first visit in four years. He was amazed at the changes he found there.[22] In place of the cowboys and horses of yesteryear, cars and tourists filled the streets. Businesses that catered to the visitors and a new, modern, three-story hotel, the Monte Vista, stood in the downtown area, drawing business away from the old, sometimes rowdy, Commercial Hotel across from the train station. Although Grey had encouraged the town's residents to take advantage of the new interest in Arizona when he visited in 1923, he was unprepared for this complete change in atmosphere and character. He had not expected the little frontier town to become a modern tourist mecca, filled with commercial lures for the tourist dollar. The small town where Grey, Buffalo Jones, and Jim Emett began their adventures, and where he was initiated into the rites of the wilderness, was most thoroughly transformed.

Grey and his guests continued on their way to the rim, where they spent a month engrossed in hunting, fishing, and exploring. A director from the Lasky film company joined the party at the lodge so he could begin to select locations for the filming of another of Grey's novels in the Tonto Rim area. Using the cabin as a base camp, Grey and his guests camped at Beaver Dam on the Tonto Creek and explored other locations on and near the rim.

After leaving Arizona in October of 1927, Grey embarked upon a year-long fishing cruise of the South Pacific islands aboard his yacht. Grey's attention was increasingly focused upon these islands, to which he was initially drawn by his love of fishing. The tropical ocean certainly provided challenge and excitement—equally significant, as Arizona and the American West became settled, Grey looked farther afield to find the wilderness he so craved. The South Pacific was relatively untouched by civilization, and Grey could encounter primitive people living with the unspoiled loveliness of nature. It was the fresh and untouched land to which he retreated as civilization relentlessly pushed into Arizona.

Grey's final visit to the state took place in the fall of 1929. He planned a tour of Utah and northern Arizona which would culminate in a stay of a month or more at his Tonto lodge. The party consisted of ten people: his son Romer, daughter Betty and a friend, secretary Mildred Smith, Robert Carney (a Scottsdale photographer), three friends from California, George Takahashi (his Japanese cook), and Takahashi's helper, J. Nasanka.[23] The entourage's itinerary included Utah's Robber's Roost near Green River, Bryce Canyon, and Zion, Arizona's Grand Canyon and Havasupai Reservation, and Flagstaff, where they planned to rest for a few days before going to Rainbow Bridge. There, he would meet Fox Studios' director R. E. Houck and select exact film locations for an upcoming production that featured the bridge as background.[24] Finally, the group would adjourn to Grey's cabin; there, Grey planned to obtain film footage he needed to supplement action he had already recorded of a bear hunt for a sport film.

Grey arranged for a camera crew to meet him at his cabin. However, when he returned to Flagstaff from the reservation and tried to make arrangements for his Tonto Basin bear hunt, he found that the game laws had been changed since his last visit to Arizona and he was a few weeks early for the opening of bear season. Since the film crew was waiting, and a delay of even a few weeks meant additional expense as well as possible failure of the project should there be an early snowfall, Grey applied for a special resident license to hunt pig-killing bears around his lodge. He met with Tom E. McCullough, the resident game commissioner. Grey expressed his regret at the late opening of bear season, and McCullough, sympathizing with his predicament, sent a telegram to the State Game Warden relaying Grey's request to hunt bear out of season.

The request was, in Grey's words, "garbled." The telegram did relay his desire to hunt bear out of season, but failed to mention the purpose of the hunt, or that the particular bear he had in mind was a rogue bear that would have to be killed anyway, probably at government expense. The State Game Warden called a meeting of the Game Commission in Phoenix to consider his application, and the request was denied. At the meeting, some of the representatives from Winslow accused Grey and his party of irresponsible hunting practices. Newspaper reporters, attracted by the association with a celebrity, sensationalized the incident. This adverse publicity, the denial of the request, the apparent betrayal by Flagstaff's game commissioner, as well as the Game Commission's evident willingness to believe the allegations of the Winslow delegation, hurt Grey deeply.

From Flagstaff, a disappointed Grey and his party traveled to the lodge and spent several weeks there "hunting with a camera." Then, a year later in the fall of 1930, Grey publicly announced his decision to leave Arizona forever. In a letter written to the Flagstaff newspaper, Grey stated his reasons for not returning to Arizona, listing several grounds for his actions. The publicity surrounding his request to hunt bear out of season prompted his decision, of course, but that was not his only reason. More importantly, he said, the forests and deserts of Arizona were being sacrificed to commercial interests: lumbermen, sheepmen, ranchers, hunters, and tourists. Tourists were taking over the beauty spots and spoiling them with their refuse. Shops, gas stations, and restaurants that marred the landscape were being built to cater to these tourists. Hunting season brought hundreds of amateurs who violated the rules of the state and the laws of compassion and wisdom in their killing. Ranchers and sheepmen wanted the deer killed so there would be plenty of graze for sheep and cattle, and the lumbermen were cutting down the forest. Money interests were fattening on Arizona's resources, and in the process were destroying the state's most precious possessions. Those agencies that were charged with protecting the natural beauties—the Forest Service and the Game Commission—were doing nothing to prevent this despoilation, according to Grey's letter. In fact, they were doing all they could to aid the despoilers. The beauty of Arizona's wilderness was fast vanishing in the face of these depredations. Grey wrote that he could not bear to watch as the Arizona he had explored, written about, and loved was destroyed. Zane Grey's association with the state would hereafter be confined to the written word.[25]

AN ALBUM

Lina Elise (Dolly) and Zane Grey, soon after their marriage in 1905.

"Buffalo" Jones, circa 1908, one of those who initiated Grey into the harshness of life on the Arizona Strip.

Mildred Smith, Grey's secretary, seated in the foreground of the Hopi ruins at Betatakin; the photo is thought to have been taken by Zane Grey, circa 1922.

Zane Grey straddles a southern Arizona desert dune.

While assisting in the 1922 location filming of *To the Last Man* in Monument Valley, Zane Grey (standing) and a companion contemplate one of the formations that gave the area its name.

On the set of *To the Last Man:* James Wong Howe, who would gain great fame as an early movie cameraman; Zane Grey; Richard Dix, the male lead, partially hidden behind Grey; Lois Wilson, the female lead; and crew members. It is thought that the man behind the camera next to Howe is John Huston.

Kneeling on a rocky Mogollon Rim promontory, Grey takes aim at a bear far below; circa early 1920s.

Grey after a successful hunt.

Two inquisitive Tonto Basin bear cubs entertain the author.

Grey and his oldest son, Romer, on a Tonto Basin hunting trip; circa early 1920s.

The restored Zane Grey hunting lodge, originally built in 1921 by the Haughts for the author's use and restored in the mid-1960s, is now a mecca for Zane Grey enthusiasts from around the world.

A letter written by Grey to his wife from his Florida fishing camp, 1924.

A G R E E M E N T

THIS AGREEMENT made this 17th day of May, 1935,
between ZANE GREY, of Altadena, California, hereinafter
called the "AUTHOR" and COLUMBIA PICTURES OF CALIFORNIA,
LTD., a California corporation, hereinafter called the
"PURCHASER":

W I T N E S S E T H:

1. The Author hereby grants and assigns to the
Purchaser, and the Purchaser hereby purchases from the Author,
all of the following rights in and to the story entitled
"OUTLAWS OF PALOUSE", written by the Author, for a period
of seven (7) years following the first release of the motion
picture photoplay which the Purchaser may hereafter produce,
based upon or adapted from the said story. The rights covered
hereby are as follows:

(a) All of the motion picture rights throughout
the world in and to, and in connection with, the said story,
together with the sole and exclusive right, subject to the
approval of the Author as hereinafter provided, to use, adapt,
change, translate, combine with other literary, dramatic and/or
musical material; arrange, transpose, add to, interpolate in
and subtract from said work in connection with the production
and distribution of one version of a motion picture photoplay
in each language throughout the world, including the right to
make silent and synchronized versions of said motion picture
photoplay; the right to project, transmit, and produce said
motion picture photoplay audibly and by the art of cinematog-
raphy, and in other present or future arts or methods of motion
picture production and distribution; the right to copy or vend,
license and exhibit said photoplay through the world, together
with the further sole and exclusive rights by mechanical and/or

The first and last pages of a 1935 contract with Columbia Pictures; it is unusual in that it is one of the very few that both Grey and his wife signed.

apply to any extraneous material used by the Purchaser, its
successors or assigns, not contained in the story as written
and published by the Author.

8. This agreement shall bind and inure to the benefit of the parties hereto, their respective heirs, executors,
administrators, successors and assigns.

9. Any and all notices or other papers which either
party hereto is required or desires to give to the other shall
be in writing. Notices or other papers shall be deemed served
if and when they are deposited in the United States Mail, or
with a telegraph company, postage or toll prepaid, addressed
to the Author at 3680 Beverly Boulevard, Los Angeles, California,
or to the Purchaser at 1438 North Gower Street, Hollywood,
California, or such other place in the County of Los Angeles
as the parties hereto may from time to time designate in
writing.

IN WITNESS WHEREOF, the parties hereto have duly
executed these presents the day and year first above written.

x _Zane Grey_
AUTHOR

COLUMBIA PICTURES CORPORATION,
a corporation,

By _Ralph Cohn_
PURCHASER

APPROVED:
ZANE GREY, INC.

By _Lina Elise Grey_
President

Edward Bowen
Secretary

-7-

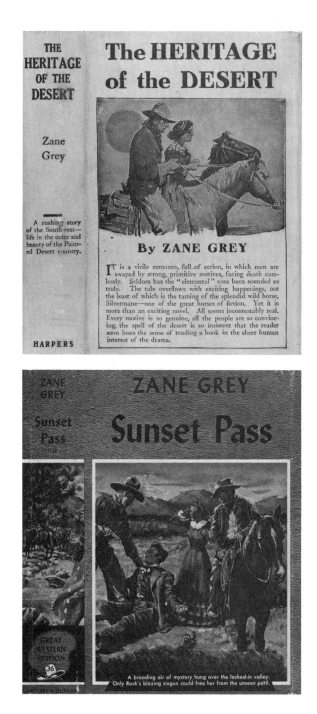

THE
HERITAGE
OF THE
DESERT

Zane
Grey

A rushing story
of the South west—
life in the color and
beauty of the Paint-
ed Desert country.

HARPERS

The HERITAGE of the DESERT

By ZANE GREY

IT is a virile romance, full of action, in which men are swayed by strong, primitive motives, facing death carelessly. Seldom has the "elemental" note been sounded so truly. The tale overflows with exciting happenings, not the least of which is the taming of the splendid wild horse, Silvermane—one of the great horses of fiction. Yet it is more than an exciting novel. All seems incontestably real. Every motive is so genuine, all the people are so convincing, the spell of the desert is so insistent that the reader soon loses the sense of reading a book in the sheer human interest of the drama.

ZANE GREY

Sunset Pass

ZANE GREY

Sunset Pass

GREAT WESTERN EDITION 36

A brooding air of mystery hung over the locked-in valley. Only Rock's blazing sixgun could free her from the unseen peril.

Original dust jackets: *The Heritage of the Desert,* published by Harper and Brothers, is described as "a virile romance . . . a rushing story of the Southwest—life in the color and beauty of the Painted Desert country." *Sunset Pass,* published by Grosset & Dunlap, sold for $2.95 in its hardcover edition; *Horse Heaven Hill,* published by Harper and Brothers, was the sixtieth Zane Grey novel to go into print and was issued in 1959, twenty years after the author's death. As the publisher's statement notes, "Harper's publication of Zane Grey books never kept pace with his terrific output. He usually completed two and frequently three novels in the course of a year . . . leaving the task of editing to Mrs. Grey." These dust jackets illustrate the stylistic evolution of the publishing industry's efforts to catch the bookbuyer's eye.

The author at his writing desk in his Altadena, California, home; circa late 1920s.

THE
LITERATURE

CHAPTER V

SAGAS OF
CANYON COUNTRY

When Zane Grey visited the Grand Canyon and the Arizona Strip, he found a land that surpassed even his imagination in beauty and desolation. Traveling with Buffalo Jones and Jim Emett, he explored Flagstaff, Lee's Ferry, House Rock Valley, Kaibab Forest, Grand Canyon and the Colorado River, and the Arizona Strip. This land and its people were, for the most part, unknown east of the Mississippi River, making it rich material for the aspiring author. Grey's first successful writing attempts used the Grand Canyon area as a setting and incorporated many of its people as characters. Later, he continued to use plots and themes inspired by the land and people of this region. Throughout his career, Grey turned to the canyon country for material and inspiration. Examination of the places, people, and themes he used in his novels drawn from Arizona's Grand Canyon area reveals three broad thematic categories into which these books can be placed: the lion hunt, the Mormon experience, and the contemporary scene.

After his first wild adventure in Arizona with Buffalo Jones in 1907, Grey returned to the East with a trove of material. During his trip, he had crossed deserts and mountains, learned to ride horses, endured sand, thirst, snakes, and tarantulas. He viewed ancient Indian ruins, stood at the rim of the Grand Canyon, met wild horse trackers, rangers, cowboys, ranchers, and Mormons, listened to and absorbed Jones's stories of the Old West, and hunted. The dangerous sport of hunting mountain lions for capture particularly caught his attention, and he wrote several books, short stories, and nonfictional accounts that utilized this theme.

The Last of the Plainsmen (1908), which Grey wrote after his 1907 trip, was intended to publicize Jones's buffalo refuge in House Rock Valley and his experiments in cross-breeding cattle and buffalo (producing an animal called a cattalo). In addition, the book was intended to prove to eastern skeptics Jones's claims of lassoing and capturing mountain lions alive; the chapters detailing the hunt are clearly the focal point of Grey's attention. He revels in action-filled description, but pays little attention to the morality of the hunt. By comparison, the buffalo refuge and the cattalo experiment fade in importance.

Grey's descriptions of the land through which he passed on his way to the great lion hunt are sketchy, but once he arrived on the north rim of the Grand Canyon, he apparently gave free rein to his descriptive talents. Although Grey had seen the canyon once before, he had never viewed it from the north rim, nor had he seen it at sunrise or at dusk. While keeping a sharp lookout for lions, Grey describes the canyon from his perch on the rim wall.

> Most striking in that vast void were the long, irregular points of rim wall, protruding into the Grand Canyon. From Point Sublime to the Pink Cliffs of Utah there were twelve of these colossal capes, miles apart, some sharp, some round, some blunt, all rugged and bold. The great chasm in the middle was full of purple smoke. It seemed a mighty sepulcher from which misty fumes rolled upward. The turrets, mesas, domes, parapets, and escarpments of yellow and red rock gave the appearance of an architectural work of giant hands. The wonderful river of silt, the blood-red, mystic and sullen Rio Colorado, lay hidden, except in one place far away, where it glimmered wanly.[1]

Passages such as this reveal Grey's talent for description, a talent that became the hallmark of his writing.

The Last of the Plainsmen was Grey's first attempt at describing the canyon. Repeatedly, he used the canyon as a setting and as a means of expressing his thoughts and feelings. Similarly, descriptions of the people Grey encountered on this first trip serve as vehicles for the expression of the author's opinions.

The only character who is convincingly developed in *The Last of the Plainsmen* is Buffalo Jones. Portrayed as an aging, yet still vital, western pioneer and adventurer, Jones appears to represent to Grey essential frontier qualities: strength, fortitude, knowledge, and wisdom. In addition to discussing Jones's buffalo preserve, cattalo experiments, and lion-hunting escapades, Grey devotes several chapters to background episodes. Jones's attempt to capture musk-ox in the Arctic and his account of the last buffalo herd are given particular attention. Jones is characterized by Grey in this book as a dreamer, motivated by benevolence to preserve many different species of native wildlife. Jones makes appearances in *Raiders of the Spanish Peaks* (1938) and *The Thundering Herd* (1925), as well; in these books, his life as a buffalo hunter and plainsman is emphasized. In other accounts, however, Grey reveals a different perception of both Jones and his particular brand of hunting.

Grey followed *The Last of the Plainsmen* with "Tige's Lion " (1908), "Lassoing Lions in the Siwash " (1908), *Roping Lions in the Grand Canyon* (1908), *The Young Forester* (1910), *The Young Lion Hunter* (1911), and *Don, the Story of a Lion Dog* (1928). All of these novels, novelettes, and short stories use the lionhunting in the Grand Canyon as both setting and plot. Each embodies a variation on the point of view or the theme.

The Young Forester and *The Young Lion Hunter* are books for children that tell the adventure of hunting wild mountain lions from a boy's point of view. "Tige's Lion" and *Don, the Story of a Lion Dog* relate the same story, but focus on the personalities and traits of the dogs that were used to hunt the lions. "Tige's Lion" describes a dog so intent on the hunt that he falls over the edge of the canyon with his teeth sunk into a lion. *Don* tells of a dog who had been mistreated by humans, Jones included, but who responds to Grey's acts of kindness with a devotion that eventually saves his life. *Don*, "Tige's Lion," *The Young Forester,* and *The Young Lion Hunter* deal with different aspects of the lion hunt, but share in the celebration of the thrill and excitement of the chase.

In several of these books, Grey raises questions concerning the morality of the hunt and the hunters. *Don* reveals the ruthlessness of Buffalo Jones, who spares no love or pity for any man or beast, and uses the quickest and most expedient means to extract the utmost from both. To train dogs to chase only lions, for example, he would fire birdshot at them when they succumbed to the temptation to chase a tantalizing rabbit. Grey attempts to express his concern for the welfare of the dogs, but the effort is to no avail.

> At first I was so astounded and furious that I could not speak. But presently I voiced my feeling. 'Wal, it looks worse than it is,' he said, with his keen gray eyes on me. 'I'm using fine birdshot and it can't do any more than sting. You see, I've no time to train these dogs. It's necessary to make them see quick that they're not to trail or chase any varmints but lions.'
>
> There was nothing for me to do but hold my tongue, though my resentment appeared to be shared by Jim and Emett. They made excuses for the old plainsman. Jim said: 'He shore can make animals do what he wants. But I never seen the dog or horse that cared two bits for him.'[2]

Numerous incidents such as this, in which Jones pushes dogs, horses, and even men to the extreme edge of their abilities, no doubt prompted Grey to refer to him on one occasion as a "fiend."[3]

Not only Jones's character, but the morality of the hunt itself is called into question in *Roping Lions in the Grand Canyon*. This novelette was billed as a juvenile version of *The Last of the Plainsmen*, yet it contains some very serious, adult-oriented themes. It describes the purpose of the hunt as to capture the mountain lions alive so that they could be transported to Jones's animal reserve and eventually supplied to zoos across the nation. During the hunt, a discussion takes place involving Jones, Emett, Owens, and Grey over whether it is less cruel to kill lions outright than to sentence them to a life in captivity away from their natural habitat. The discussion is prompted when a lion hurls himself over the canyon's edge to avoid capture. Grey and Owens favor outright killing, while Jones and Emett believe that "life, even in captivity was preferable."[4]

This discussion assumes a different nature when, later, another lion meets his death as he tumbles over the canyon's rim, fighting to the last, with his captor's rope tightly encircling his neck. Their efforts to lift him back over the edge of the precipice strangle him. The nobility of the lion's struggle for freedom prompts Grey to make Jones say, uncharacteristically, "We've been fools. . . . The excitement of the game made us lose our wits. I'll never rope another lion." The remarks attributed to

Jones are not only out of character, but are, according to Grey himself, impossible for most men to accomplish. The hunt had caused him to reflect on the nature of human dominance and to conclude sadly that "men are still savage, still driven by a spirit to roam, to hunt, and to slay."[5]

While a good hunting trip was one of Grey's chief pleasures in life, he occasionally harbored some doubts about the sport. During his Arizona trips and his other visits to the West, he stalked mountain lion, deer, elk, wild turkey, and bear; he also captured animals alive, although he acknowledged that death might be more merciful to the animal than a lifetime in captivity. He was most concerned, however, with the effect of hunting on the hunter. In 1917, he wrote about a hunting trip in the Colorado Rockies.

> The more I hunt the more I become convinced of something wrong about the game. I am a different man when I get a gun in my hands. All is exciting, hot pressed, red. Hunting is magnificent up to the moment the shot is fired. After that it is another matter. It is useless for sportsmen to tell me that they, in particular, hunt right, conserve the game, do not go beyond the limit, and all that sort of thing. . . . It is a question of spirit, and men who hunt are yielding to and always developing the primitive instinct to kill. The meaning of the spirit of life is not clear to them.[6]

In other nonfiction accounts of hunting trips, notably the article entitled "Arizona Bear" in *The Country Gentleman* (December 1920), Grey again ponders the pleasure derived from hunting and killing. He concludes that it is an inheritance from the primitive past, an inborn trait that cannot be eliminated or ignored. Although it remains an expression of a savage nature, Grey rationalizes his enjoyment of the sport by saying that an occasional return to primitive pursuits is necessary to strengthen mind and body for the perpetual struggle of life.

Grey's attitudes toward hunting, animals, and the West were also greatly influenced by Jim Emett, a member of the 1907 hunting party. Emett, the Mormon pioneer in the Arizona Strip who operated Lee's Ferry, was first encountered by Grey in Flagstaff in the spring of 1907; Emett was on trial for cattle theft at the time. After his acquittal, Emett joined Grey and Jones on the first leg of their journey to the north rim of the Grand Canyon. When they reached Emett's ranch, he decided to remain with the two men and participate in the lion hunt.

Grey referred to Emett in a magazine article as "the man who influenced [him] most."

> All Western men, developed by hard contact with the desert, are great whether they are good or bad. But Emett was good, and he typified all that was rugged, splendid, enduring. He was an old Viking of the desert. My debt to him is incalculable. No doubt he exerted more influence over my development, creating, all absorbing love for the Southwest than any other Westerner.[7]

Emett's life seemed to exemplify qualities and values that Grey absorbed and emulated.

According to Grey, Emett taught him three things. The first was a love for the West and its beauty, color, and grandeur. Grey acknowledged that this one gift was the most significant as far as his future writing was concerned. It was this love that taught Grey to observe the western terrain and to recreate it for his readers. These descriptions are the hallmark of his work.

Grey also learned love of all living creatures, particularly horses, from Emett.

> I first saw Silvermane, the famous white-maned stallion, wildest of wild horses, when I was with Emett. I saw many others, and once Emett thought surely he had got me a glimpse of Wildfire. How the old gray-headed westerner would stand and gaze! To be sure, he wanted to capture those incomparable wild stallions, but I believed it was because he loved them. Whatever it was, I absorbed it in addition to my own thrilling emotion.[8]

Magnificent, brave, resolute horses are featured in almost all of his western romances. In the novel *Wildfire* (1917), the central figure is a horse. This tale is set in the Lee's Ferry region, on an oasislike ranch near the Colorado River crossing which differs little from Grey's description of Emett's domain. The story climaxes with a wild race between Wildfire and another horse, Sage King, both pursued by a fire that is nipping at their hooves.

The Last of the Plainsmen includes an episode in which Grey, Jones, Emett, and the rest of the party are joined by the Stewart brothers of Fre-

donia (the Stewarts were Mormons and professional wild-horse trackers). The party pursues a legendary wild stallion, the White Mustang,
down Nail Canyon, managing only to catch a glimpse of him. The
Stewart brothers reappear as characters in a short story entitled "Lightning," which was not published until 1975. In this version, the brothers
track the wild horse of title from Fredonia to central Utah, finally aban-
doning their task of killing him for bounty money; instead they want the
glory of capturing and owning him.

Years later, in 1924, when J. Frank Dobie, as secretary of the Texas
Folk-Lore Society, was collecting stories for a volume of Texas legends,
he noticed a marked similarity between Grey's account of the White
Mustang and a number of legends, all dated approximately 1840, concerning what was referred to as "the pacing white stallion," or "the steed
of the prairies" by old plainsmen.[9] The story seemed very similar to a
legend submitted to him by Walter Prescott Webb entitled "The White
Steed of the Prairies," and Emerson Hough's use of the legend in his book,
North of '36.[10] Dobie sent an inquiry to Grey, who quickly replied:

> I am afraid I cannot lay claim to any legendary origin for the
> horses of my stories. They were inspired, of course, by bands of
> wild horses which I have seen.[11]

Grey used the majestic wild stallion many times, usually with some
slight variations, and horses play an important role in almost all of the
western romances.

The last lesson Emett taught Grey was that of endurance. He learned
this through the example of Emett's life, which he characterized as
filled with

> loneliness, hunger, thirst, cold, heat, the fierce sandstorm, the
> desert blizzard, poverty, labor without help, illness without
> medicine, tasks without remuneration, no comfort, but little
> sleep, so few of the joys commonly yearned for by men, and
> pain, pain, always some kind of pain.[12]

This lesson, Grey stated, encouraged him to continue with his writing
despite early failure. Grey owed a great debt of gratitude to Emett for his
example of the finest that the West was capable of producing.

Despite this admiration, Grey could not develop the same feeling for

Emett's religion, Mormonism. He applauded much of what the religion represented and readily acknowledged the drama of the early Mormon struggles; he used Mormons as characters and Mormonism in the plots and themes of many of his early novels. Yet, though Grey tried very hard to understand the religion and explain it to a hostile world, the deeper his investigation went, the more he encountered principles, attitudes, and practices he could not endorse. Paramount in his explanation of the Mormon experience was an attempt to understand how the religion and the community had interacted with the frontier environment, and how they had changed and been changed by the West. *Heritage of the Desert* (1910), *Riders of the Purple Sage* (1912), and *The Rainbow Trail* (1915) trace Grey's initial regard for Mormonism, his later rejection of it, and his eventual reconciliation with those Mormon tenets that he admired.

Heritage of the Desert is Grey's most sympathetic treatment of Mormonism. Set in northern Arizona and southern Utah, near the Colorado River, it tells the story of an ailing easterner who comes West and is given refuge by the Mormons. With their aid, he regains his strength, and becomes involved in their struggle against cattle rustlers and dishonest ranchers who are trying to drive them off their land.

One of the major characters in *Heritage of the Desert* is a tall, impressive patriarch, August Naab. Naab, a thinly veiled Jim Emett, owns a ranch that is literally an oasis in the desert. He also maintains the Colorado River crossing entitled by Grey "The Crossing of the Fathers."[13] Grey describes the ranch as

> an oval valley, level as a floor, green with leaf and white with blossom, enclosed by a circle of colossal cliffs of vivid vermilion hue. At its western curve the Colorado River split the red walls from north to south.[14]

Compare those words with Grey's actual description of Jim Emett's ranch.

> Emett's home was set at the edge of a luxuriant oasis, green with foliage and alfalfa, colored by bright flowers, and shut in on three sides by magnificent red walls three thousand feet high. The thundering Colorado formed a fourth side and separated the oasis from another colossal wall across the river.[15]

From the description of August Naab's fictional home, a stranger could easily identify Emett's settlement at Lee's Ferry.

The physical description of Naab is also almost identical to that of Emett. Naab is characterized as

> close to threescore years, his chest was wide as a door, his arm like the branch of an oak. He was a blacksmith, a mechanic, a carpenter, a cooper, a potter. . . . He was a farmer, a cattleman, a grafter of fruit trees, a breeder of horses, a herder of sheep, a preacher, a physican. Best and strangest of all in this wonderful man was the instinct and the heart to heal . . . anything hurt or helpless had in August Naab a friend.[16]

Grey describes Jim Emett in "The Man Who Influenced Me Most," in almost the same words he used to depict Naab. He commented on his height, his build, his unkempt hair and beard, his mastery of numerous different trades, and his power of revelation and healing, stating, "anything crippled, hurt, lost, deserted, or sick found refuge with Jim Emett."[17] Clearly, Emett was the model in creating the fictional character of August Naab.

Some of Emett's family members became part of Naab's family as well. Emett's eldest son, Snap, appears as Snap Naab, a dissolute drinker and wife-beater who eventually meets his end in a gunfight over a woman. This unflattering portrait resulted from Snap Emett's rebuff of both Grey and Jones. Grey states in "The Man Who Influenced Me Most," that he "grew friendly with all these sons except the eldest, and he never had any use for Buffalo Jones or me." It was never wise to snub Zane Grey!

Another member of August Naab's fictional family is a man named Dave Naab. This relatively minor character is evidently patterned after David Dexter Rust, a Mormon pioneer and explorer of Kane County, Utah. Rust was a member of both the 1907 and 1908 hunting expeditions, and Grey made arrangements for him to serve as guide on the 1911 trip, but they were unable to meet as planned. Grey reveals the relationship between Naab and Rust in a letter to his Utah friend.

> Of all the criticisms of my book [*Heritage of the Desert*], and I have received thousands, I like yours best. You can gamble that if the story stood the test you gave it, it has the stuff. I shall pub-

lish a few paragraphs of your letter, with your permission, and also that I drew the character of Dave Naab from Dave Rust. This will appear in New York papers and you need not mind the publicity.[18]

Although the character of Dave Naab plays a minor role in the story, it does reveal how Grey incorporated the people he met on his western trips into his fiction.

Grey applauded Mormonism's emphasis on the work ethic and on family life, but was quick to point out the discordant note of polygamy. He stated his opinions through the main character in *Heritage of the Desert* who, when invited by August Naab to become a Mormon replied:

> I feel—differently from Mormons about—about women. If it wasn't for that! I look upon you as a father. I'll do anything for you. Your work, your religion, your life—Why! I've no words to say what I feel. Teach me what little you can of them, August, but don't ask me—that.[19]

Polygamy was the one practice and principle that Grey found most disturbing about Mormonism, even in his gentlest treatment of the topic.

Conversely, *Riders of the Purple Sage* is a harsh indictment of Mormonism, one which centers on the practice of polygamy, but includes Grey's contempt for narrow-minded fanaticism of any type. It is set almost exclusively in southern Utah, yet its critique of Mormonism links it to Grey's Arizona experiences, as he encountered Mormon culture and society on his trips into Arizona. In this novel, the Mormon hierarchy, representatives of law and order, are corrupt, and the anti-establishment figure of the gunman, Lassiter, exhibits all the noble traits.[20] Jane Withersteen, the main character, is a wealthy Mormon woman whose property, body, and soul are coveted by the hierarchy. Lassiter and Jane combine their forces, but are unable to thwart Mormon ambitions. They are forced to flee for their lives, hiding in an inaccessible canyon, Surprise Valley.

The Mormon men in this story are almost uniformly hardened, cruel, and greedy. They represent authority gone mad with power, allowed to grow unchallenged in their isolation. Their traits are traced to their experience of religious persecution. As Jane Withersteen states: "The men of my creed are unnaturally cruel. To my everlasting sorrow I confess it. They have been driven, hated, scourged till their hearts have hardened."²¹ Nevertheless, these traits represented for Grey the worst element of Mormonism: stern, unforgiving and unreasoning people who could not deviate from established ways and ideas.

The Mormon woman, always a favorite with Grey, is portrayed as a meek, gentle, and sad individual. Forced to submit to their husbands' will in all matters, these women endure the offensive custom of polygamous marriage. Lassiter, the Mormon-hating gunfighter, seems to be speaking for Grey when he says, "I believe Mormon women are the best and noblest, the most longsufferin', and the blindest, unhappiest women on earth."²² These women, according to Grey, are victims of polygamy, a system that serves only to increase the power of men. In any book in which Grey approaches the topic of Mormonism and polygamy, he expresses sympathy and kindness toward Mormon women, but antagonism toward Mormon men. In accentuating the men's rigidity and the system of polygamy, *Riders of the Purple Sage* represents Grey's most strident attack on Mormonism.

The Rainbow Trail, sequel to *Riders of the Purple Sage,* presents another of Grey's views on Mormonism. This tale is again set in extreme northern Arizona and southern Utah, yet it incorporates as well many features of another of Grey's Arizona regions, the Navajo Reservation. It is the tale of another defeated easterner, John Shefford, who comes west to track down a legend told him by a friend, Venters, a character from *Riders of the Purple Sage.* According to the legend, Lassiter, Jane Withersteen, and Fay Larkin, a young girl whom Jane has adopted, are still living in Surprise Valley, isolated from the world. Shefford wants to find the hidden valley, help Lassiter and Jane escape, and marry Fay Larkin, sight unseen. In this quest, he is befriended by an Indian trader named Withers, who employs him as his agent to take supplies to tiny northern Mormon hamlets. Accompanied by an Indian, Nas Ta Bega (Nasja Begay), and a Mormon, Shefford learns the Mormon ways and discovers, to his astonishment, that the towns he visits are communities where plural wives are common.

The book's setting incorporates several areas Grey visited on his early trips into the Arizona Strip. During his 1908 expedition, small Mormon communities were of particular interest to him, and in planning the 1911 excursion he specifically intended to return to some of these Mormon villages, mentioning Fredonia and Kanab by name.²³ Fredonia is included in *The Rainbow Trail* as an example of a community where polygamy reigns. Surprise Valley and Thunder River, other places Grey discovered in 1908, are incorporated into his novels. Surprise Valley appears in *Heritage of the Desert, Riders of the Purple Sage,* and *The Rainbow Trail,* while Thunder River appears for the first time in *The Rainbow Trail.* These locations, familiar to Grey through his early visits to the Arizona Strip, also provide the setting for the latter, Grey's third novel concerning the Mormon experience.

The story line of *The Rainbow Trail* takes place in 1889, twelve years after that of *Riders of the Purple Sage.* In the time that had passed, the Mormons were confronted by several new circumstances: the federal government passed laws exacting severe penalties for polygamy, forcing polygamous husbands to hide from the law; increasing numbers of non-Mormons (or Gentiles as they were called) moved into the Mormon-dominated area, which required Mormon tolerance and exposed them to foreign ideas; and, finally, the dogmatic first-generation Mormon patriarchs were growing old and their numbers were decreasing.[24] They were replaced by younger men with less unyielding convictions.

This combination produced changes in the religion's nature. Grey's treatment of the subject in *The Rainbow Trail* incorporates those changes, and dwells upon the same two elements—polygamy and fanaticism—he so severely criticized in *Riders of the Purple Sage.* Grey also introduces a critique of Mormonism within a critique of organized religion in general.

Grey continued to portray polygamy as a moral and social evil. In *The Rainbow Trail,* however, he modifies his position on the severity of its immorality. In an introspective passage, he has the main character, Shefford, consider polygamy.

> If they [plural wives] were miserable, they certainly did not show it, and the question came to him how just was the criticism of uninformed men? His judgement of Mormons had been established by what he had heard and read, rather than what he knew. He wanted now to have an open mind. . . . One wife for one man—that was the law. Mormons broke it openly; Gentiles broke it secretly. Mormons acknowledged all their wives and protected their children; Gentiles acknowledged one wife only. Unquestionably the Mormons were wrong, but were not the Gentiles more wrong?[25]

Grey thus expressed his own realization that what the Mormons did openly, others did secretly, while criticizing Mormon practices. Indeed, his doubts concerning the immorality of plural marriage may well have stemmed from his own changing lifestyle, as it was during the period 1914 to 1916 when evidence of Grey's associations with women outside of marriage was first appearing in the media.[26] Grey could not quite bring himself to endorse polygamy, just as he could not endorse similar practices among nonpolygamists, but he seemed to indicate that the Mormon way was slightly more honorable.

Despite this more tolerant attitude toward polygamy, Grey maintained that it was destined to disappear. While Mormonism existed on the frontier, isolated from the mainstream of American life, it could flourish, but when civilization reached the Mormon communities, bringing with it laws and customs of a more settled society, polygamy would no longer be allowed.[27] Mormons who supported it were themselves increasingly influenced by ideas of the outside world and turned against it, even as stricter laws made it more difficult to practice.

Nowhere did Grey more explicitly express this changing nature than in the courtroom scene of *The Rainbow Trail*. In this episode, those women suspected of participating in polygamous marriages are on trial in an effort to prove that their husbands are practicing polygamists. The courtroom is filled with concerned and curious citizens. As Grey describes it:

> There were many stalwart, clean-cut, young Mormons of Joe Lake's type, and these men appeared troubled, even distressed and at a loss. There was little about them resembling the stern, quiet, somber austerity of the more mature men, and nothing at all of the strange, aloof, serene impassiveness of the gray-bearded patriarchs. These venerable men were the Mormons of the old school, the sons of the pioneers, the ruthless fanatics. Instinctively, Shefford felt that it was in them that polygamy was embodied . . .[28]

In this book, the younger men, influenced by modern ideas and attitudes, question older practices. It is they who bring more flexible, tolerant, and humane ways to their religion. Through them, Mormonism adapts to the changing times, losing its sterner and more peculiar fea-

tures and aligning itself with mainstream America. This maturation ena-
bles the church to survive in the modern, complex world, yet once it
loses its unique features, according to Grey, it is no different than any
other organized religion, having the same strengths and weaknesses as
all the rest.

Grey found in Mormonism what he felt was the fatal flaw of all organized religion. Polygamy was not the real problem, nor was the un-
bending fanaticism of its early founders. Its weakness lay in its purpose.
The Rainbow Trail contains Grey's expression of his attitude, with Shefford's observation.

> Strikingly it had come to him that the fault he had found in
> Gentile religion he now found in the Mormon religion. An old
> question returned to haunt him—were all religions the same in
> blindness? As far as he could see, religion existed to uphold the
> founders of a Church, a creed. The church of his own kind was a
> place where narrow men and women went to think of their own
> salvation. They did not go there to think of others. . . . Was there
> no religion divorced from power, no religion as good for one
> man as another, no religion in the spirit of brotherly love?[29]

In this strong indictment, Grey states that all religions have a tendency to
become inward-looking and clannish, to set themselves apart from other
groups, and to regard themselves as unique and superior. The convictions that had initially generated the religion become lost in an effort to
perpetuate the institution and its leaders. Grey saw Mormonism adopt
this pattern after losing its frontier peculiarities and as the fervor of its
founders died out.

In tracing the history of the Church of Jesus Christ of Latter-Day
Saints, Grey sketched the effect of the frontier environment on its society, character, and ideas. *Heritage of the Desert* portrays the Mormons'
early struggles to exist and maintain their religion and society in the
primitive West. Survival of the fittest was the law, as Grey saw it. Mormons learned how to best survive within the wilderness by practicing
that law. They adopted the tactics of desert animals who survive in the
severe environment, and they learned to place the welfare of the group
above that of the individual. These lessons produced men like Jim
Emett, who personified to Grey the best that the West and Mormonism
had to offer. They also engendered a system that exploited the weak.

Riders of the Purple Sage illustrates the effect of the West's isolation on a community. Seclusion from the rest of the world allows those in power to become tyrants, creating self-perpetuating and exploitive systems such as polygamy. *The Rainbow Trail* demonstrates the group's evolution and maturation. As civilization reaches outlying Mormon areas, the harsh religion softens and modifications are made to fit it within the modern world. The Mormonism that Grey saw during his trips to the Arizona Strip retained the strong traditions of its pioneer forefathers, but it also possessed the flexibility and progressiveness necessary for twentieth-century life.

Grey's travels also alerted him to the unique challenges presented to the Arizona Strip by the modern world. Among these were questions concerning the area's role in national and world events, issues relating to the welfare of the region's wildlife as human population pressures increased, and concerns about the impact of technological advances. Grey's interest in the area prompted him to express his misgivings and offer his advice in several romances set in the contemporary Arizona Strip.

Call of the Canyon (1924) uses Oak Creek Canyon, Flagstaff, and the Grand Canyon as settings of a story that uses the disillusionment and materialism that emerged after World War I and the nation's shocking neglect of its veterans as themes. Carley Burch, a wealthy eastern debutante, goes to Arizona to retrieve her fiancé, a veteran who had been wounded and was attempting to regain his health in the West's invigorating atmosphere. Carley is initially indisposed to find anything likeable about the region; her only desire is to bring her fiancé back East. During her stay, however, her feelings change, and she perceives the West's value to herself and to the nation. Carley's growing appreciation is based upon her perception of eastern society's artificial nature when compared to the primitive, yet vital, western life.

Comparisons of eastern society and values with those of the West constitute a recurring pattern in Grey's portrait of Arizona. The East is represented as materialistic, artificial, hedonistic, and dissipated, while the West is strengthening, rejuvenating, and formative of such Turnerian virtues as independence, self-reliance, courage, honesty, and purity. Easterners are either weak, ill, or downright villainous in Grey's books, while westerners are forthright, plain, sometimes crude, but always sincere. The rare western villain is only on the nether side of the law temporarily, misled, or influenced by eastern greed. Villains always come to their senses, express remorse for their crimes, and become new people. Whether the juxtaposition is set in the past or in the present, the decadent East suffers and is overwhelmed by western virtue and simplicity. Grey uses this pattern to illustrate his conception of the nature of the West. To him, it was the repository of American strength, virtue, and values.

Grey's main character in *Call of the Canyon* faces numerous ordeals, both physical and emotional, which tax her endurance and strength. In overcoming these challenges, she discovers the strength of her own character. Her experiences mirror Grey's own early encounters. He, too, was a tenderfoot, a dentist who wanted to be a writer; not wealthy, but certainly used to a middle-class standard of comfort. When he described a character developing the strength and endurance the West required, he was essentially writing of his own experiences. Grey wrote Dolly from Arizona that:

> It has taken me over a month of hard work—awfully hard work—to get back into a physical condition such as I used to have, but I have succeeded. I cannot remember when I ever looked so well. I was fat. Now I am hard, and still seem to keep the flesh I gained, and I have gotten into a condition of mind comparable to the physical.[30]

The strengthening power of the western environment, stimulated in large part by the necessity for hard, physical labor to survive, formed a crucial theme in Grey's depiction of Arizona and the West. In *Call of the Canyon,* hard work, simplicity, and contact with the out-of-doors—demanded in the West but available anywhere—are portrayed as values that would put America back on the right path. Old values were easily identifiable in the West, where the past walked side-by-side with the present. From his earliest visits to Arizona, Grey was captivated by the presence of cowboys, Indians, horses, and automobiles, all on the same Flagstaff streets. They provided an exotic blend, and gave early twentieth-century Arizona towns their unique personalities. In this way, Arizona towns differed little from other western frontier towns, which had the modern world hot on their heels. Grey incorporated this intermingling in his novels, creating a portrait of a developing and changing West and illustrating virtues that, in his opinion, America should strive to retain.

This injection of modern elements into the frontier setting, and the changes they caused, presented other novel problems for the Arizona Strip. Foremost among them were extraordinary pressures on the region's wildlife, caused by human intrusion into a vast but fragile wilderness. Grey's concern for the animals of the Arizona Strip is dramatically illustrated in his novel, *The Deer Stalker* (1925). This novel emphasizes (through its focus on the plight of starving deer on the north rim of the Grand Canyon) the disasters caused by human attempts to manipulate the balance of nature. Reduction of natural predators—particularly mountain lions—through bounties demanded by ranchers in an effort to reduce attacks upon domestic stock resulted in tremendous growth in the deer population. The herd became so large that by December 1924 it faced starvation; north rim forests could not support their great numbers. In an attempt to alleviate the problem and avoid allowing hunters to shoot the almost-tame animals, a plan was devised to drive the deer through the Grand Canyon and into the forests of the south rim. These events and their results are presented through the main characters of Grey's romantic novel, Thad Eburne and his fiancée, Patricia Edgerton.

The drama of the ill-fated deer drive and the romance of the two characters is acted out against the majestic backdrop of the Grand Canyon. Throughout the novel, the canyon is used to set both scene and mood. It is also clear that, as late as 1924, when this novel was written, Grey was still experimenting with description of the canyon. In *The Deer Stalker,* he gives free rein to his imagination and descriptive talents, portraying the canyon in reverential awe.

> She approached the rim as if it were an altar. She looked. The great gap seemed to yawn at her. Lights, shadows, distances of the morning had now vanished. The canyon was filled with a smoky haze, through which the millions of red lines and surfaces shone with softened accents. . . . Here was a shrine for the lonely soul, where one could face its agony or revel in its exaltation.[31]

The Grand Canyon assumes a spiritual nature in Grey's description, as it did each time he tried to convey its impact in words. Using it as a part of the setting allowed him to display his talent for drawing word pictures and his ability to weave together setting, plot, and theme.

As well as the Grand Canyon, Grey wrote about other natural features of the Arizona Strip and northern Arizona in *The Deer Stalker*. He includes the San Francisco Peaks, Sunset Peak, Painted Desert, the Little Colorado River, Kaibab Forest, and Flagstaff. He points out specific features of the Grand Canyon itself, notably Jacob's Ladder, Devil's Corkscrew, Indian Gardens, Bright Angel Canyon, and Marble Canyon. Wrapping up this portrayal is his account of the Colorado River.

A favorite item in Grey's collection of natural wonders, the Colorado River makes an appearance in eight of his novels and articles and is always described in roughly the same fashion.[32] Grey found nothing peaceful or exalting in this powerful ribbon of water. He emphasized its size, treachery, and roar, and he likened its reddish, silt-colored flow to blood. Most of all, he was intrigued by its power and capacity for destruction. It seemed the height of folly for feeble persons to attempt to harness that river, but when the attempt was made, Grey made sure he was present to witness it.

Construction of Hoover Dam began in 1931, more than a decade after the project was initially conceived. Because of his long fascination with the Grand Canyon and the river that created it, Grey could not let the opportunity to record its taming pass. Throughout the early years of construction, he visited the site several times, talked with workers and engineers, and collected information for a book set in the confusion, optimism, and hard work of raising a dam against the surging Colorado.[33]

Boulder Dam (1963), is the story of a young man who discovers his abilities and gains self-respect through employment on the dam project. In the process, he aids a young girl who has escaped from white slavers. The novel is set in the Boulder City–Hoover Dam area and contains accurate and detailed accounts of the towns of Las Vegas and Boulder City, as well as the construction process. Even the accounts of gambling in Las Vegas's Block 16 (the red-light district) and the episodes concerning the white slavers are based on information Grey collected through personal experience and interviews with Las Vegas's early law enforcement officers.[34]

The attempt to harness the Colorado River through technology forms the thematic backdrop for this novel. Grey begins the story with a prologue that consists of a brief history of the Grand Canyon and the Colorado River and emphasizes the immensity of the project.

In our modern day men even more daring then Coronado and Powell stood upon the black rim of the lower canyon and conceived of the cliff dwellers, or of the dreaming red-skinned savage, an idea born of the progress of the world, as heroic and colossal as the inventive genius of engineers could conjure, as staggering and vain as the hopes of the builders of pyramids, an idea that mounted irresistible despite the mockery of an unconquerable nature—and it was to dam this ravaging river, to block and conserve its floods, to harness its incalculable power, to make it a tool of man.[35]

The story ends with an epilogue that includes a look at the completed dam and a vision of the area five hundred thousand years in the future. According to Grey's "vision," the dam is gone, humanity itself has disappeared, and all that is left is "the rapacious river, augmented to its old volume, no longer red but dirty white, remorseless and eternal." Human technological accomplishment might hold back the river for a time, but, according to Grey, the river will eventually be victorious.

Throughout his work based on the Grand Canyon and the Arizona Strip of the 1920s and 1930s, Grey displayed three primary concerns. He wanted his readers to recognize the promise that the West held for the rest of the nation as the repository of American characteristics and values. He wanted, as well, to alert his readers to the threat to wildlife of the region as increasing numbers of people arrived. Finally, he was inspired by the Hoover Dam project to explore the impact of modern technology on the West, concluding that, as the forces of nature were much stronger than the power of humankind, it could have only a temporary effect. In each of the books dealing with the modern West, regardless of the particular concern he dramatized, Grey emphasized the value and beauty of the land, the wildlife, and the people.

The Arizona Strip, the Colorado River, the Grand Canyon, the north rim forests, the cowboys, and the Mormons provided Grey with a wealth of material, and Grey utilized the themes, characters, plots, and settings that he discovered in the Arizona Strip territory again and again. Gradually, though, even his inventive capability was exhausted. When this became apparent to him, he turned his attention toward the literary expression of another area of Arizona, another facet of the West: the northern reservations of the Navajo and the Hopi.

CHAPTER VI

THE RESERVATION
BOOKS

Zane Grey's adventures on the Indian reservations of northeastern Arizona began in 1911 and extended intermittently through 1929. He made seven visits, stopping at points of interest and meeting the residents, both Indian and Anglo. He was particularly impressed with the Kayenta trading post, Monument Valley, Navajo Mountain, Paiute Canyon, and the Rainbow Bridge, as well as with Indian traders, such as John and Louisa Wetherill, and the Indians themselves. Grey incorporated what the locale offered in the way of characters, setting, plot, and theme into a number of novels, novelettes, and nonfictional articles. These centered on the Indian experience, stories treating the Anglo on the reservation, and tales accentuating the physical setting.

Al Doyle introduced Grey to the Arizona reservations; as well as showing him the natural attractions, Doyle entertained Grey with stories of life in the West, one of which Grey used as a basis for the novel *The U.P. Trail* (1918). This story chronicled the construction of the first transcontinental railroad, with which Doyle had been associated. When Doyle's story, embellished by Grey, was published, Grey wrote to Doyle:

I am sending you a copy of *The U.P. Trail,* the Union Pacific story you always wanted me to write. I have mentioned your name in the dedication. This is a big book, and my best. I'll bet it makes you sweat.[1]

Doyle proved to be a valuable source of stories, information, and eyewitness accounts. He had an intuitive grasp of what would interest Grey. He escorted the author to the reservations and introduced him to the people who lived there.

Most fascinating of these people were the Native Americans themselves, including Hopis, Paiutes, and Navajos. The Navajo Indians impressed him the most, but he developed a kindly regard for Paiutes as well. The Hopi, with their more sedentary lifestyle based on agriculture, were neither as mysterious nor as interesting as the more nomadic and warlike tribes. Navajo customs and beliefs, and their difficulties adjusting to the reality of Anglo dominance, most intrigued Grey, but he was appalled at the problems of all of the tribes. This concern inspired several novels set in that locale, which would capture the experience of the Indians, especially the Navajos, as well as expose conditions on the reservation.

One of the books, and the most comprehensive in dealing with the Indians' situation, was published with the title *The Vanishing American* (1925). This novel is the story of an Indian boy, Nophaie, who is abducted at the age of seven from the reservation by misguided Anglos. He is educated in the East, attends Carlisle Indian Industrial School, and gains fame as an athlete. He returns to the reservation after an eighteen-year absence with a desire to regain his identity as a Navajo (or Nopah, a literary label Grey used) and a commitment to apply what was beneficial from his Anglo education to help his people. Grey traces Nophaie's trials from 1916 through the years of World War I and the disastrous influenza epidemic that swept across the reservation during the fall and winter of 1918 and 1919. He describes the wartime fluctuation of the wool market, a major tribal economic base; the Navajo support of and participation in the war; and the dissension between Navajos, the federal government, and missionaries. In detailing this brief history of the Navajo people, Grey was able to express a number of his ideas and opinions concerning the American Indian.

As the title of the novel suggests, Grey was convinced that the American Indian, as a distinct group, was disappearing. He makes this opinion clear a number of different times in passages similar to the following:

> The white race will never wholly absorb the red. If that were possible it might be well for both. But the Indian will merely be pushed back upon the barren lands and eventually swept off the earth. These things we strive against, as the Nokis fight being cheated out of their water and land, or as our efforts to save Gekin Yashi—these things are nothing but incidental to the whole doom of our people. . . . We must resist, but the end will come, just the same.[2]

According to Grey, Nophaie's education caused him the agony of perceiving the Indian's destiny. In dramatizing this point of view, Grey reflected society's prevailing attitudes as well.[3]

In *The Vanishing American,* Grey examines the issue from several angles. He continues to endorse the idea that the Indians were a dying race (although the census of 1920 belied it), and expands the theme with some thoughts on the manner in which they would disappear.

> The Indian's deeds are done. His glory and dream are gone. His sun has set. Those of him who survive the disease and drink and poverty forced upon him must inevitably be absorbed by the race that has destroyed him. Red blood into the white! It means the white race will gain and the Indian vanish.[4]

Grey also conjectured about the result of this blending. Nophaie, who succumbs to his love for a white woman and marries her, realizes that his children will be only half-Indian and that their distinct Indian identity would eventually be submerged by the Anglo. The mixing of the two races would result in the loss of the Indian traits, Grey concluded; his belief in the innate superiority of the white race was the basis for this opinion.

Many of Grey's comparisons of the Indian and Anglo were rooted in the popular assumption of evolutionary progress. He theorized that Anglos were a bit further along the evolutionary path than were Native Americans, and based his supposition of white supremacy on that thought.

As he saw the beauty of this wild, lovely land, and the rugged simplicity of the Indian, his marvelous endurance, his grand childlike faith in the supernatural and the immortal, so likewise he saw the indolence of this primitive people, their unsanitary ways of living, their absurd reverence for the medicine man, their peculiar lack of chastity—and a thousand other manifestations of ignorance as compared with the evolutionary progress of the white man. Indians were merely closer to the original animal progenitor of human beings.[5]

In Grey's opinion, the supposed Anglo superiority was not always a boon, nor was the Indians' conjectured inferiority always a burden. Consider the following passage from the same book:

If the red man was inherently noble, a dreamer of the open, a fighter of imaginary foes, a warrior against warrior of another tribe, a creature not meant for civilization, then the white man was a step above the Indian in evolution, past the stage of barbarism, steeped in a material progress of the world, selfish and intellectual, more pagan than the Indian, on the decline to a decadence as inevitable as nature itself.[6]

Progress cost the white race much of value, while the Indian retained many worthwhile traits. Nevertheless, when the two races were combined, primitive Indian characteristics would be overwhelmed by more advanced Anglo culture.

Grey did not seem to really believe that the two races would ever blend, any more than he thought the Indian would survive. In a letter to the *Ladies Home Journal* in 1922, in which magazine *The Vanishing American* first appeared in serial form, he wrote:

I feel certain that the sympathy of all true Americans will go out to the redman in his trial. This novel is concerned with the soul of the Indian. The great mass of busy Americans do not know the beauty and nobility of the Indian as he exists still where unspoiled by contact with a materialistic civilization. They do not realize that he has been cruelly wronged, that he will never be absorbed by the white race, than [sic] he is vanishing from the earth.[7]

Grey's use of the phrase "true Americans," (an apparently unintentional irony) made it clear that whether he was writing fiction or nonfiction, he had a highly romanticized view of the Native American. Magnifying their virtues and sufferings and smoothing over their faults, he presented the American public an entirely sympathetic image and appealed to the emotions of his readers. In doing so, he softened the Indians' supposed doom by indicating that their fusion with the Anglos would allow them to retain the best that both races offered, and save them from total annihilation.

Grey's discussion of interracial marriage in *The Vanishing American* was completely unacceptable to American society in the 1920s. The original serial publication in *Ladies Home Journal* created quite a stir among readers, who found the idea of a white woman marrying an Indian man repugnant. Consequently, Grey's editors at Harper and Brothers asked him to adjust the ending, eliminating the marriage, before the story was issued in book form.[8] In the 1925 edition, and in subsequent editions, Nophaie, the main character, dies at the end of the book under circumstances inconsistent with the plot.

Time has not proven Grey's theories concerning the fate of the Indian to be correct. Far from diminishing in numbers and disappearing, or being completely assimilated into the Anglo culture, the Navajo remain a distinct group within the United States and their numbers are increasing rapidly. They have adopted many Anglo ways, but retain their separate identity. Still plagued with the problems of poverty, alcohol, and disease that Grey lamented, the tribe has nonetheless made considerable advances beyond the society the author observed in the early twentieth century. Although Grey's ideas appear somewhat naïve when viewed from the vantage point of the 1980s, it should be remembered that he went beyond most of the liberal thinkers of his time in considering interracial marriage as a solution. Most would only go so far as to recommend acculturation for the Indian.

Acculturation was projected to occur through education, but Grey felt there were numerous flaws in this plan. Indian schools were intended to teach Native American children to speak English, wear Anglo clothes, be a farmer or have a trade, have Anglo values, be a Christian—in short, to be imitation Anglos, the goal of acculturation. Often established and managed by religious groups under the auspices of a distant federal government, the schools were usually staffed by teachers who were either tremendously overworked or not of the highest caliber.

Students were forcibly removed from their homes and sent long distances to boarding schools, where they were taught that their parents' beliefs and way of life were wrong, and were ridiculed and punished for any lapse into Indian ways.

After some years of this, Indian boys and girls were returned to their homes. Their long absence, strange ways, and ignorance of their peoples' customs caused them to be alienated from their own society, yet an Anglo education had not prepared them for a place in Anglo society, even if the whites had been willing to accept them. The result was neither assimilation nor acculturation, but rather, the sad plight of a person caught between two cultures, accepted by neither.

Three of Grey's novels—*The Vanishing American, Captives of the Desert, and Wild Horse Mesa*—address problems posed by this system. Each reveals a slightly different facet, yet in each, the theme of cultural conflict is readily apparent. A sampling from these novels reveals the depth of Grey's awareness of and concern for these very real problems.

In *The Vanishing American* the issue comes to a head in several places. At one point, Nophaie expresses his feelings in the following manner:

> How immeasurably far apart he felt from the people who lived there! Everyday brought more bitter proof. When he conversed with Indians he used their language, but when he thought, his ideas were expressed in his mind by words of English. . . . That was Nophaie's tragedy: He had the instincts, the emotion, the soul of an Indian, but his thoughts about himself, his contemplation of himself and his people were not those of the red man.[9]

The irony of the story lay in the distance between Nophaie and his people, which was created by his Anglo education. Before his help was accepted, he had to prove himself to be truly a Navajo.

Grey, in *The Vanishing American*, indicated that education might not be entirely bad for the American Indian. The system had flaws, of course, but it had benefits as well.

> By a process of elimination Marian arrived at a few proofs of the compulsory school education being beneficial to the Indians. Perhaps ninety-nine out of one hundred students returned to the old life, the hogan and the sheep. They could not help but carry

ideas of better life, better methods, better management. They could understand English and knew the value of money and of a trade. So that whether they liked it or not they were somewhat better equipped to meet the inroads of the white man.[10]

It was inevitable, Grey implied, that the Navajo would increasingly come into contact with the Anglo. Education would provide them with the preparation to better meet the challenges of cultural contact.

The effects of Anglo education were mentioned in another reservation novel, *Captives of the Desert*. First issued as a serial in *McCall's Magazine* in 1925, its setting included several locations on the Hopi and Navajo reservations, such as the Hopi pueblos, Tuba City, Red Lake, and Kayenta.[11] The focus in this book, though, is less on the Indian theme than on the love story between the two main Anglo characters. Nevertheless, questions concerning the Indian provide a thought-provoking aspect to the novel.

The cultural tug-of-war is symbolized by the Anglo-educated Navajo girl, Magdaline, who plays a minor but intense role in the story. Her education made her dissatisfied with traditional Navajo life, but not quite acceptable to the Anglos. In one lengthy passage (shortened here where appropriate), she expresses her problem:

> I forgot the hogan, ill-smelling to those who were no longer used to it. I forgot the customs of my people—the sheep killed before the hogan and immediately served half-cooked. I forgot that they slept on the ground with sometimes no blanket beneath them. I forgot that living close to animals breeds lice and pests for the body. . . . They are satisfied as they are. And they are strangers to me. They watch me with half-distrust as they would an unknown white woman. My education had made me an outcast. My people have no place for me; and what place has the white man? I can go to his towns and cities and be a servant in the homes, paid much less than a white servant.[12]

An educated Navajo, this character perceives the primitiveness of her people, but is powerless either to change their lives or to escape.

This theme is reemphasized in *Wild Horse Mesa* (1924). Although this novel is set in Utah and involves Paiute Indians, it is applicable to the Arizona situation as well. Again, the character who experiences and expresses cultural conflict is a female who had spent nine years in a government school. Upon her return to the reservation, she finds that her only future is as the wife of an Indian who already had one wife.

In this novel and in *Captives of the Desert,* Grey differentiates between the experience of an Indian female and an Indian male.

> Indian boys who are educated go back to the dirty habits of their people. We girls learn the white peoples' way of living. We learn to like clean bodies, clean clothes, clean food.[13]

The point is stated even stronger in *Captives of the Desert* when the character Magdaline states:

> And because he loves me, I will be supposed to love him and go to his hogan and kill sheep to half-cook for him. Where are your eyes not to see that education makes no difference to the men of my race? They go back quickly to old customs. But I am a girl— a woman. I am altogether different. I could go back, yes, like a slave. But what would it do for me? Some of the girls go back and seem happy. Yes, they are happy in losing one leg to have the other. Some people are that way.[14]

The educated Indian girl caught between two cultures in this way had even more serious problems in Grey's stories. She often became easy prey of unscrupulous white men, as indicated in both *Wild Horse Mesa* and *Captives of the Desert.* These characters would seduce her and lead her to a tragic end, usually death. Whether the educated Native American was male or female, severe obstacles were encountered in finding a niche in society.

Another theme that attracted Grey was that of Native American religion and the impact of Christianity on that religion. Navajo and Hopi beliefs are discussed in three of Grey's reservation novels—Hopi practices in *Captives of the Desert,* and those of the Navajo in *The Rainbow Trail* and *The Vanishing American.* In each of these treatments, Grey demonstrates a profound reverence for the beauty and symmetry of their spiritual beliefs. Because *The Rainbow Trail* does not concentrate upon the Indian theme, its treatment of religion is brief, hardly more than an attempt to outline the relationship of belief structures and the Navajo way of life, complete in three pages. It is in *The Vanishing American* that a detailed treatment appears.

Grey was particularly impressed by the way the Navajo lived their beliefs. One particular passage describes Grey's perception of the Navajo faith:

> He thinks in symbols. His God is Nature. The Indian feels God in sensorial perceptions of an immense and mystic spirit of life and death about him. All that occurs in nature are manifestations of a supreme being's control of the universe. To these he prays and chants. . . . All the phenomena of nature have direct and personal connection with the Indian's inner life. His head is in the clouds. He walks with shadows. He hears the silent voices. He is mystic.[15]

Balancing this romantic view is another sequence in which Grey's depiction is more graphic:

> The Nopahs [Navajos] prayed to the Sun, Moon, Stars, Wind, Thunder, Lightning—anything beyond their understanding and all of which they symbolized. They recognized the unseen power which sent the sun each day, and the warm winds and the cold, and all physical phenomena. They heard the idea that God was a person and abided in a particular place, but they argued if there was a personal God and a material heaven, there would be a road leading to it. They believed there was a physical life for spirits of the good, which belief accounted for their custom of sending with the dead the best horses, bridle, saddle, belt, beads, gun. Tools of all sorts were sent—the spirits of the tools—everything that was sent along for the spirit of the dead man had to be killed so that they could go along. Nopahs believed that spirits of evil persons went into animals here on earth—into the coyote, bear, cougar, snake—and this was the reason why the Indians seldom or never killed these creatures.[16]

Neither passage is derogatory of the native religion; both reveal Grey's reverence for it. He was most impressed by the way in which the religion was a part of everyday Navajo life, the way in which their beliefs were deeply rooted in an observation of the natural world, and the way the environment had shaped these beliefs.

When Grey wrote of the connection between Indian religion and nature, he was, to a great extent, expressing his own religious views, also firmly rooted in a love of nature.[17]

> For Nophaie saw clearly that nature was the great law. The Indian, even the barbarian, was nearer the perfection that nature worked so inscrutably for. The individual must perish that the species might survive. Nature's ideal was strength, virility, fecundity, long life, all physical. If nature was God then the only immortality of man lay in his offspring.[18]

Interwoven with this love of nature was an endorsement of Spencer's Social Darwinism. Nature ruled all, and worked incessantly to achieve its ends through the survival of the fittest. This natural law was most clearly observable on the frontier, Grey implied, where its forces were unhindered by the contrivances of a civilized society. The passage quoted above typifies Grey's opinions, the point of view he expressed in so much of his literary output. The religion of the Navajo spoke to his own beliefs, and thus found a receptive observer who portrayed it in the most complimentary light. Grey's perception was that the religion was complete, symmetric, harmonious, and an apt expression of the Navajo's life in the desert. Grey was anxious that the religion remain pure, untouched by the white man.

Also crucial to his portrait of the Indian and his religion was a consideration of Christianity's impact on the Navajo. Introduced through missionary activity on the reservation, Christianity was also endorsed through the school system. Many reservation schools were established and staffed by religious groups, and even government schools in the early twentieth century were operated by representatives of an assortment of denominations. The groups met with little success in their conversion efforts. Their activities, so closely interwoven with the anglicizing attempts of the schools, often produced confusion and individuals who were cultural misfits.

Two of the reservation novels dramatize this impact of Christianity on the Native American. *The Rainbow Trail* and *The Vanishing American* both contain strong indictments of the interjection of Christianity into native beliefs, or more accurately, the attempt to replace native religion with Christianity. Of primary concern in these two treatments are the Indians' reactions to Christianty and the struggle that occurred when the Indian was forced to choose between Christianity and his native beliefs.

The Rainbow Trail contains a most poignant statement of the problems presented when missionaries began their attempt to convert the Native Americans. For the most part, the older Indians did not understand the new religion, nor did they care much for it. Because of their greater resistance, proselytizers turned their attention to the younger generation, often removing them from the influence of the home to boarding schools, where they were to be educated, anglicized, and converted. The removal of the young worked a hardship on the older ones left behind, as they no longer had the benefit of their labor. In *The Rainbow Trail,* a young girl, Glen Naspa, is removed from the hogan of her elderly relative by a missionary who wants to convert her. The old man does not understand what has occurred, but is afraid to be left alone without resources. His repeated refrain was, "Me no savvy Jesus Christ! Me hungry! . . . Me no eat Jesus Christ!"[19] Grey's dramatic portrayal of the confusion and concern of the elderly Navajo mirrored anxieties felt by the older Navajo generation concerning the activities of the missionaries, observed while on his visits to the reservation. Even this faded in significance, however, when Grey considered the individual who struggled to reconcile traditional beliefs with what he was taught about Christianity.

In *The Vanishing American* the main character attempts to accommodate both the Christian beliefs he had been taught and the native religion he remembers. Long years at the Anglo schools had eroded his faith in his people's gods and caused him to view their practices as superstition, but the bitterness he feels toward the whites who had robbed him of his heritage prevents him from accepting the Christian God. At the beginning of the novel, Grey introduces this conflict when he portrays Nophaie's feelings.

> I tried to return to the religion of my people. I prayed—trying to believe. But I cannot. . . . I am an infidel! I cannot believe in the white man's God. . . . My white teaching killed it. That is the curse of the missionaries. The Indians' religion is best for him. The white preacher kills the Indian's simple faith in his own God—makes him an infidel—then tries to make him a Christian. It cannot be done.[20]

After a long struggle, Nophaie reconciles his beliefs, becoming a Christian because "there is only one god . . . for my race, for yours, for all peoples! . . . For it is through Christianity that one gets the clearest conception of God. But He belongs not to race or creed, but to all humanity." The ending is unrealistic and not truly representative of the Navajo reaction to Christianity, but it appealed to Grey's audience. Much more realistic is the main character's turmoil as he searches for a religious identity.

The clash of religious beliefs was only one portion of the tragic image of the Native American that Grey presented to his readers. In addition to the complex question of religion, Grey also painted a picture of a conquered race who would eventually disappear, but whose death was hastened by the infusion of alien values and knowledge and the attempt of newcomers to alter the native way of life. As Grey visited the reservation, he met many Anglos engaged in bringing their culture to the Navajo and was intrigued by their lonely life and by their relationship with the Indians. As he concerned himself with the reaction of the Native American to the white man, his education, and his religion, he could not fail to notice the drama of those who were the instigators of change. The Anglos he met on the reservation were missionaries, government agents, and traders. These representatives of Anglo culture appeared in the reservation novels, often incorporated into Grey's indictment or approbation of their activities.

The group that received Grey's most severe criticism was the missionaries. Generally suspicious of organized religions and of their agents, Grey had attacked the Church of Jesus Christ of Latter-Day Saints, as well as other unspecified churches, in earlier novels.[21] Given his attitudes, it was predictable that the men who represented established religions on the reservation should come under his stern scrutiny.

Most missionaries in the reservation novels are characterized as greedy and corrupt, and sometimes cruel or vicious as well. They appear to be more interested in exploiting the Indian for their own profit, cheating him out of his land and water, or seducing young girls in their care than in saving souls. Grey's most severe critique of missionaries is found in *The Rainbow Trail* and *The Vanishing American*. The representation of missionaries in these two is consistently negative and serves as a vehicle for Grey to express personal opinions as well as expose some of the abuses of the reservation system. The appraisal of the missionaries in *The Rainbow Trail* is less strident than that found in *The*

Vanishing American, but the author casts them in a most unfavorable light in both cases.

The book, *The Rainbow Trail,* begins with a scene in which a missionary attempts to force his attentions on a young Navajo girl as a means of enticing her to leave her people and attend his school. He is thwarted by the appearance of the main character, but he pursues the girl throughout the rest of the book, and eventually persuades her to leave with him. Toward the end of the novel, she returns home, where she dies giving birth to the missionary's child. The tone throughout the novel leads the reader to conclude that the missionary's behavior was by no means exceptional, and that most reservation missionaries employed similar means.

The Vanishing American criticized missionaries in an even less subtle way, as Grey included some very strong statements in connection with their activities. These were so severe that his publishers had him remove many of the more explicit passages after the novel's publication as a serial in *Ladies Home Journal;* run in 1922, it created a public outcry. Grey felt that his exposé of missionary activities put his life in danger when he next visited the reservation.[22] His concern may have been justified, considering the reaction that observations such as the following must have generated: "of all the white race, Indians hated most the missionaries—those men who lied in one breath and preached Jesus in another."[23] In many ways, the entire novel could be considered an indictment of attempts to convert the Indians, as well as of the caliber of the men who were sent to perform this task. The novel traces the efforts of the main character to counteract harm done to him by well-meaning missionaries in depriving him of his identity and his heritage. Additionally, Grey used the novel to expose corruption on the reservation; the main character observes the machinations of evil men who call themselves missionaries. It was the presence of such men who prevented the system from accomplishing any good, Grey felt, because they created distrust of all missionaries.

Halfway through the novel, Grey pauses in the story line to analyze why the missionary system was riddled with corruption, and concludes that eastern agencies were too lax in inspecting and regulating their representatives. Because of their title, it was assumed that those men were above reproach and "could do no evil."[24] Consequently, evil or incompetent men gained positions as missionaries, and even when there was ample evidence of their intransigence, they were allowed to continue in office and perpetuate their crimes.

Another factor in the failure of the missionary system, as Grey saw it, was the reservation's isolation. Not only did this isolation ensure that flaws would not be immediately observed, but also had a negative effect on the character of the missionaries themselves. A passage from *The Vanishing American* illustrates this point:

> Least of all do the majority of those missionaries, good and bad, understand the desert and its meanings, its subtle influence upon life, its inscrutable ruthlessness and ferocity.
>
> . . . Always in sparsely uninhabited places, especially in wastelands where the elements make life stern, men and women find self-interests and human weaknesses growing magnified. They go back in the scale of progress.
>
> . . . Whatever missionaries might have been in civilization, out in the wild country they are confronted with life in the raw. They react to it just as subtly as other men. The only reason they are more culpable then other men is because their office as ministers of the white gospel gives them a peculiar opportunity and advantage, which to use is utterly base.[25]

It is interesting to note Grey's emphasis on the power of the environment to shape human behavior. Time and again, regardless of which region he addresses, he returns to this theme. Missionaries were no less susceptible to the influences of the land about them than were others. Because they were far away from well-regulated activities of more densely populated areas, their own convictions of right and wrong could blur. Surrounded by a people who did not share their heritage and moral system, missionaries lost grip of their identity and purpose on the reservation, responding to the primitive influence of isolation, and falling prey to their own animal natures. On the reservation, isolation was a prime factor in the corruption of those who came to convert the Indian to Christianity, but it did not affect all missionaries in the same way—for some, the environment enhanced positive traits.

As examples of these successful individuals, Grey used missionaries who were motivated by an unselfish desire to aid humanity. Those that he singled out were of various religious affiliations, as Grey professed loyalty to no one denomination. What impressed him most was an emphasis on teaching practical knowledge rather than religious conversion.

Mormon and Catholic missionaries are mentioned in *The Rainbow Trail* and *The Vanishing American*. Jacob Hamblin, a Mormon, is cited in *The Rainbow Trail;* Grey praises him for his early work among the Navajo who, at that time, were as warlike as any southwestern Indian group. Hamblin traded with them and taught them useful skills and gained their friendship for Anglos. In *The Vanishing American,* Grey speaks of Catholic priests "who at least were kind and helped the Indians, and who perhaps came nearer to real missionary work."[26] Grey was impressed by motives and work, if not always by achievement.

Even the best of the missionaries faced incredible obstacles to making any progress toward their desired goals. Grey also indicated through his writing that their tasks were impossible to accomplish; much of what they did succeeed in doing, in defiance of all odds, created only more misery for the Indian, Grey concluded. He sums up their problems thus:

> The good missionary, the one of a thousand, the man who leaves home and comfort and friend to go into a lonely hard country, burning with zeal to convey the blessing of Jesus Christ to those he considers heathen—armed with a printed book and full of tract speeches, the platitudes of preachers, the "words of religion"— honest and sincere and confident—this missionary has little or no conception of the true nature of his task, of the blindness with which he is afflicted and must eradicate, of the absurdity of converting Indians in little time, of the doubtful question as to the real worthiness of his cause, and, lastly, of the complications fomented by other missionaries, and employees of the government, the cliques, the intrigues, the inside workings of the machine. . . . The good missionary's life is a martyrdom, his fight against the parasitical forces noble as it is futile, and his task of transforming the Indian's religion of nature to the white man's creed one well nigh impossible.[27]

Good missionaries were so few and their tasks so monumental that even Grey, no lover of organized religions or their agents, respected their efforts. His appraisal of the immensity of their tasks and the problems they faced was a reasonably accurate representation of actual conditions on the Indian reservations during the years that he visited there. Few in number, an even smaller number were really dedicated to their role. The system itself was inefficiently organized, the Indians were resistant to their message, they had only meager financial support, and above all, the worth of the goal was questionable.

Underlying all other negative factors was this great question: was the attempt to convert the Indians to Christianity a valuable one? Both novels that address the missionary system in depth, *The Rainbow Trail* and *The Vanishing American,* question the consequences of such actions, but it is in *The Rainbow Trail* that Grey's most concise statement of opinion on the matter appears.

> In the beginning the missionaries did well for the Indian. They taught him cleaner ways of living, better farming, useful work with tools—many good things. But the wrong to the Indian was the undermining of his faith. It was not humanity that sent the missionary to the Indian. Humanity would have helped the Indian in his ignorance of sickness and work, and left him his god. For to trouble the Indian about his god worked at the roots of his nature.[28]

Because Grey perceived the close association between the Indian and his religion, he realized that to change the religion was to alter the nature of the Indian. The tragedy of the missionary system was that it tried to carry out the intent of prevailing public philosophy, which was that the Indian must learn to be a white man.

Another group of Anglos on the reservation who were involved in the attempt to reform the Indian were agents of the United States Bureau of Indian Affairs. The agent was the representative of the federal government and was supposed to execute directives of his superiors, whose offices were in Washington, D.C. Grey spent less time in characterizing agents than he did missionaries, but what he did write was not flattering. In general, the agents were described as incompetent or ineffectual men who were appointed to the position because of their political contacts or for other equally illogical reasons, and who accepted because of the opportunity to carve personal empires on the reservation. They often found the job beyond their capabilities, and were regarded as failures by both Anglos and Indians. The government agent is a minor character in *The Vanishing American,* in league with corrupt missionaries to exploit the Indians and to perpetuate his own power. The agent in the story is more the missionary's puppet than his co-conspirator; his incompetence makes him vulnerable to the missionary's manipulations.[29]

A third category of non-Indian reservation resident was the trader. These men received the Indian's products of wool, blankets, pottery, or jewelry and traded for groceries, cloth, tools, and other items. There were two types of traders: those that were employed by the government, and those who had government licenses but operated independently. The agency trader was usually located in the vicinity of the government agent's headquarters, while the independent operator established trading posts in outlying areas. Traders performed functions and filled a role that no other reservation group was capable of fulfilling.

Traders were often the best-liked Anglos on the reservation. They extended credit, which helped the Navajo survive economic crises, and encouraged them to produce articles that would appeal to the developing tourist trade, creating a new market for their crafts. While traders were not primarily interested in helping the Indian imitate the Anglo way of life, the relationship that flourished was a more effective process of acculturation than either the agents or the missionaries had devised. Additionally, the trader, especially the independent trader, was interested in cultivating the Indians' business. To attract the Indian, he had to establish a reputation for honesty and affability—dishonest traders did not last long.[30] The Indians soon discovered those who were unfair, and took their business elsewhere. Some of the traders went beyond what their role prescribed and made efforts to alleviate the worst conditions on the reservation. These individuals listened to problems, settled disputes, gave advice, served as mediators between the Indians and the government agents, and in general behaved as the Indians' friends and advocates.

On his initial trip to the reservation, Grey was introduced to John and Louisa Wetherill, the couple who operated the trading post at Kayenta. The Wetherills had lived on the Navajo reservation since 1906, and Louisa had personally undertaken a study of the Navajo. She spoke the language fluently and was something of an expert on tribal customs. Louisa entertained Grey with accounts of the Indians' troubles with missionaries and government agents, and told him of Navajo customs and Navajo religion. Tribal legends were also recounted.

Many of Grey's reservation novels were inspired by stories told him by Louisa Wetherill. The substance of *The Vanishing American* grew from problems that Grey heard from Louisa Wetherill, and the same issues found in *The Rainbow Trail* undoubtedly had their source in Louisa's stories.[31]

One of Grey's particularly appealing novelettes, *Blue Feather* (1961), is based upon a Navajo legend that Louisa told Grey.[32] *Blue Feather* involves a race of tall, light-skinned, warlike people from the north who enter the area where the "cliffdwellers" live. According to the story, the strangers from the north send a spy, the son of a great chief, to corrupt and weaken the city dwellers, but as he resides there, he falls in love with a maiden. The girl is the daughter of the chief of the town and queen of a neighboring village. The illegitimate daughter of the outcast queen (it is never fully explained why she was outcast, but apparently the union was spurious) is carefully hidden in a secret kiva, never seeing the light of day. The spy discovers the maiden and they fall in love. He betrays his people to save her, and she betrays hers to save him. When the northerners pillage the city and kill almost all the people, they allow the girl and her lover to live, thus letting the blood of the old ones mingle with their own.

Elements of this story bear some resemblance to the historical facts surrounding the entrance of the Navajos to the Southwest. The Navajos moved into the area from the north around 1500 and encountered Pueblo Indians, who lived in earthen towns. Navajos are taller and somewhat lighter-skinned than Pueblo Indians. These similarities seem to indicate that *Blue Feather* is an embellished version of an oral legend that describes Navajo arrival in the Southwest and their relationship with the established residents. Louisa had been told the story by the Navajo and later gave Grey a typed copy.[33]

As well as providing Grey with material, John and Louisa frequently appear as characters in the reservation books. Their most prominent role is in *The Vanishing American,* where their name is Withers and they run the Kaibab trading post. They are also in *The Rainbow Trail,* again as the Withers, traders at the Kayenta post. Grey's description of the Withers in *The Rainbow Trail* is clearly modeled on the Wetherills:

He had lived at Kayenta for several years—hard and profitless years by reason of marauding outlaws. He could not have lived there at all but for the protection of the Indians. His father-in-law had been friendly with the Navajos and P[a]iutes for many years, and his wife had been brought up among them. She was held in peculiar reverence and affection by both tribes in that part of the country. Probably she knew more of the Indians' habits, religion and life than any white person in the West. . . . His nearest neighbors in New Mexico and Colorado were a hundred miles distant and at some seasons the roads were impassable.[34]

The Wetherills surface again in *The Lost Pueblo* (1954), as the kindly Bennetts who operate a trading post, and as the Westons who run Black Mesa trading post in *Captives of the Desert*. Grey's characterizations show them to be kind, honest, concerned, capable, and amiable. Their lonely but exotic life on the reservation made them ideal material for Grey's romances.

Occasionally, Grey varied his portraits and created a villainous trader. Some of the traders, albeit not the legitimate ones, concoct plans to sell liquor to the Indians on the reservation in *Captives of the Desert*. The trader in *Black Mesa* (1955) is a thoroughly despicable Mormon polygamist who sells the Indians alcohol and cheats them. Grey's writing reflects reality in that profoundly crooked traders appear only infrequently in his reservation novels.

Missionaries, government agents, and traders constitute Grey's fictional portrait of the Anglos who lived on the reservation. From time to time, characters of a slightly different type appear, such as cowboys, government employees, or visitors from the East. But for the most part, the Anglos he wrote about fell into one of these three major categories. Each carried with it its own particular characteristics and issues. When Grey wrote about the missionaries, he emphasized his concern over the type of people they were and the effect of their work on the Indians. When he discussed the government agents, he stressed the overwhelming futility of their task, regardless of the agent's competence. He modeled almost all of the traders after the Wetherills, emphasizing their role as advocates of the Indians' cause. Regardless of which category he wrote about, he accentuates his firmly held belief that all humans were shaped by the West.

Places, always very important in Grey's writing, became a hallmark of his work. In the reservation novels, the locales sometimes assume a prominent role in the story.

The Rainbow Bridge was the reservation's most impressive landmark as far as Grey was concerned. He visited it first in 1913 in the company of John Wetherill, and once wrote:

This rainbow bridge was the one great natural phenomenon, the one grand spectacle which I had ever seen that did not at first give vague disappointment, a confounding of reality, a disenchantment of contrast with what the mind had conceived.[35]

Nonnezoshe, or the Rainbow Bridge, was also the focus of several nonfictional articles.

The giant natural bridge assumed symbolic significance to Grey. In *The Rainbow Trail,* "Nonnezoshe—The Rainbow Bridge," and "What the Desert Means to Me," Grey used the same words and phrases to express the sense of permanence the bridge gave him.

I realized that long before life had evolved upon the earth this bridge had spread its grand arch from wall to wall, black and mystic at night, transparent and rosy in the sunrise, at sunset a flaming curve limned against the heavens. When the race of man had passed it would, perhaps, stand there still.[36]

In the works, he insists that the stone edifice possessed a spirit, and in *The Rainbow Trail* he calls it the spirit of God. In *The Vanishing American* and "Down Into the Desert," the sense of permanence is replaced by an awareness of change. The bridge would perish in time, he wrote, but it had already endured countless millions of years. These two works define the bridge as a spiritual symbol of nature, freedom, solitude, and endurance. All the literature that uses the bridge represents it as the greatest deity of the Navajo. That Grey often used the same material several times to describe and interpret the bridge does not detract from the impact the great stone monument had on him.

It is impossible to discuss Grey's literary treatment of the Rainbow Bridge without mentioning the Paiute Indian, Nasja Begay. This man guided the first Anglo expedition to the bridge in 1909 and guided the Grey-Wetherill party in 1913. The Indian's role as guide is not neglected in any of the nonfictional articles on the bridge, and in *The Rainbow Trail* Nasja Begay is a minor but important character, although he is labeled a Navajo rather than a Paiute, and his name is changed to Nas Ta Bega. Grey's description of Nasja Begay reflects his reverence for the Native American and concentrates all the positive qualities of the race in this one representation.

Another reservation locale that provoked Grey's literary talents was Monument Valley. This land of wind-eroded buttes is in northeastern Arizona, completely within the Navajo Reservation, and stretches across the border into Utah. Much of *The Vanishing American* is set in Monument Valley, and the area is used, as well, in *Captives of the Desert, Wildfire,* and *Stranger from the Tonto.* The latter, published in 1956, is set primarily in Utah in the vicinity of Hole-in-the-Rock on the Colorado River. The Indian reservation is included because the main character travels from Tonto Basin country to Utah, and crosses Monument Valley on his return trip at the end of the novel. Foremost in Grey's descriptions of Monument Valley are the colors of the area, the resemblance of the buttes to better-known phenomena, and the eerie sense of death and decay that clings to the monuments.

Ruins of past civilizations, found everywhere on the reservation, intrigued Grey as well, but he liked best of all a ruin that he named Becky-shibita.[37] This particular site is featured as the setting in *Lost Pueblo,* a romance centering upon a spoiled, eastern flapper and a serious young archeologist. Beckyshibita is also mentioned in *Stranger from the Tonto* as a stopping place on the trail to Utah, and is associated with Keet Seel Ruin. The nonfictional account of Grey's 1922 excursion along the Paiute Trail to Rainbow Bridge, "Down Into the Desert," mentions the ruin as Becki-shib-iti or Cow Water, and locates it about ten miles north of Red Lake Trading Post. Most likely, the fictional setting of Becky-shibita is a combination of Keet Seel Ruin and Cow Spring Canyon, which are both close to a trail identified on the map as the Rainbow Trail. Whatever the inspiration of the fictional Beckyshibita, Grey's inclusion of prehistoric ruins shows his fascination with these remnants of earlier civilizations, as well as his efforts to make his portrait of the reservation as true to life as possible.

Other places on the reservation are frequently highlighted in Grey's works. Red Lake Trading Post, with its unique octagonal building, is featured in *Captives of the Desert, The Vanishing American,* and *Stranger from the Tonto,* as well as "Down Into the Desert," and the trading post setting of *Black Mesa* bears a strong resemblance to Grey's nonfictional description of the Red Lake Post. The Kayenta post is described in *The Rainbow Trail, The Vanishing American, Captives of the Desert,* and *Lost Pueblo.* Tsegi Canyon is renamed Deception Pass and written into *Riders of the Purple Sage,* published only one year after Grey's first visit to the reservation. The Little Colorado River, the

Painted Desert, the Hopi villages, Moencopi Wash, and Tuba City are also mentioned briefly in several works. These additional features add local color and a sense of detail and authenticity to the works.

The literary works Grey developed from his trips to the reservation accentuate differing aspects of reservation life. In some works, the drama of the Indians' life is unfolded, with its struggle to accommodate the presence of the Anglos. In other books, the lonely existence of the Anglos on the reservation is explored, and the life of missionaries, government agents, and traders is scrutinized and critiqued. In still others, the natural setting is highlighted. Regardless of the human drama told, or the facet of reservation life stressed, the overriding thematic consideration of the reservation novels is an exploration of the influence of the natural environment on human behavior and character. This theme continues in Grey's literary studies of the extreme southern deserts of Arizona, as he once again examines the power of the desert to shape human behavior and character.

CHAPTER VII

STORIES OF THE BORDER

G rey discovered the deserts of southern Arizona in the spring of 1912, when he visited the region in search of a setting for a story idea given him by a friend, Robert Hobart Davis, editor of *Munsey's Magazine*.[1] Alive that spring with the intrigue of revolution, the border between Arizona and Mexico offered ample material for inspiration.

The revolutionary president of Mexico, Francisco Madero, was threatened by Pascual Orozco, who had formerly supported him. General Huerta, leader of Madero's army, chased Orozco out of Mexico and into Arizona, despite the United States troops who patrolled the border. Amidst this turmoil, Grey expected to find both setting and material for a romance. Later, his expectations fulfilled, Grey produced two novels set in the ferment of the Mexican Revolution, and a sequel, written much later. Additionally, several short stories reflect his fascination with the desert. The literary output of this period accentuates several topics related to the Mexican-American border: the revolution itself, Mexicans, Yaqui Indians, and Anglo-American cattle ranchers of the region. Into these topics was woven Grey's basic conception of the West, the effect of the environment on humans.

The two early novels, *Desert Gold* and *The Light of Western Stars*, both published in 1913, are set in different borderland sections, although both use the Mexican Revolution as a backdrop. The story of *Desert Gold* takes place directly along the border, with the action moving west from Douglas and Agua Prieta to Altar Valley, Sonoyta, Papago Wells, and the Sonoran Desert at El Camino del Diablo. *The Light of Western Stars* moves away from the immediate border and into the mountains of southeastern Arizona. The Peloncillo Mountains, which span Arizona and New Mexico, the Guadalupe Mountains of extreme southwestern New Mexico, and the Chiricahua Mountains are mentioned, as is Cochise Stronghold, located in the Dragoon Mountains. The San Bernardino Valley between the Chiricahuas and the Guadalupes plays a part, as does Aravaipa Canyon, northeast of Tucson. The detailed accounts Grey developed are fairly accurate, although distances are often altered for effect. Grey also incorporated regional history in the plots, adding detail and color.

Desert Gold is the tale of a young easterner, Richard Gale, a failure in his father's business. He comes to the West in search of adventure, and finds it immediately upon his arrival in a border town, as he rescues an aristocratic Spanish girl from revolutionary ruffians, and takes her to safety at an isolated ranch in Altar Valley. There, he promptly falls in love with the rancher's stepdaughter, Nell. As the rancher is a U.S. Inspector of Immigration, Gale is immediately drafted to be a border ranger, but as the revolution grows more intense, he, the Spanish girl, her husband (who was also Gale's friend), an Indian called Yaqui, and several others are forced to flee into the Sonoran desert. References to Madero, Orozco, and Huerta are liberally sprinkled throughout the narrative; this gives an air of authenticity, unsupported by explicit historical detail or interpretation.

The revolution plays a similar role in *The Light of Western Stars,* which centers upon a wealthy young woman, Madeline Hammond (nicknamed Majesty) who comes to the West, ostensibly to visit her black-sheep brother. She falls in love with the desert, as well as with Stewart, a drunken cowboy who is the first person she meets as she steps off the train. Majesty then purchases a cattle ranch and proceeds to remodel it into a replica of New York City's Central Park, complete with golf links. As revolutionary activity draws closer, her cowboy lover is reformed by her influence and becomes an honorable and trustworthy man.

Previously involved in skirmishes on Madero's side, Stewart had been awarded hero status by Mexican forces on both sides. To save Majesty from further humiliation—for, though she does not realize it, she is legally married to the cowboy—he rejoins Huerta's army and is captured by the insurgents and sentenced to death. When Majesty finally discovers her love for Stewart and her status as his wife, she moves south to prevent his execution. Again, references to Porfirio Diaz, Madero, Orozco, border guerrilla activity, the flow of arms into Mexico from the United States, and possible United States intervention are scattered throughout the novel; the events of those early violent years, from Diaz's fall to Madero's victory and Orozco's revolt, are sketched in fairly accurate fashion, though not in great detail. Although the revolution is more tightly woven into the plot in *The Light of Western Stars* than in *Desert Gold,* in both novels it serves as a backdrop only. The books were essentially love stories.

While Grey enthusiastically utilized the Mexican Revolution for drama, action, and historical setting, he was personally biased against Mexicans. His characterizations of them, like most of his descriptions of ethnic groups, are complex and sometimes contradictory. He developed two stereotypes, one of which emphasized traits of cunning, arrogance, and cruelty, and the second, which stressed ignorance and laziness.

The ruling class was linked to its Spanish ancestry. Grey admired what he called the "true Spanish," and wrote of them in a laudatory fashion, "Like all the Spanish—the real thing—she's made of Damascus steel."[2] The "true Spanish" could trace their ancestry to Spain and had no Indian blood in their veins. Mexicans, on the other hand, had only a portion of the Spanish inheritance, the more negative traits at that, unmitigated by nobility. Spanish influence on the Mexican character surfaced in their predilection for intrigue, Grey felt.

> Oh, these Mexicans are subtle, mysterious! After all, they are Spaniards. They work in secret, in the dark. They are dominated first by religion, then by gold, then by passion for a woman.[3]

Their penchant for cruelty was another way in which Mexicans revealed their Spanish nature. Countless incidents in these southern Arizona novels portray Mexicans in acts of ruthlessness and barbarity. In *The Light of Western Stars,* Grey epitomizes this trait in the concluding passage of the novel.

Montes was ceremonious, gallant, emotional. Madeline saw his pride, and divined that the situation was one which brought out the vanity, the ostentation, as well as the cruelty of his race. He would keep her in an agony of suspense, let Stewart start upon that terrible walk in ignorance of his freedom. It was the motive of a Spaniard.[4]

Occasionally, Mexicans demonstrated what Grey considered to be positive Spanish traits, electrifying acts of courage and loyalty. More often, though, pride, arrogance, cunning, and cruelty appeared, and were always confined to Mexicans of the upper social and economic classes.

The other side of the picture surfaced in Grey's depiction of the lower classes. In these people, called Mestizos, the Spanish heritage was overpowered by the mixture of Spanish and Indian blood. The Mestizos were noted for their laziness, ignorance, slovenliness, vice, and defeat by the hostile environment. Grey describes a Mexican village in *The Light of Western Stars* in the following way:

She had not believed such squalor could exist anywhere in America. The huts reeked with filth; vermin crawled over the dirt floors. There was absolutely no evidence of water, and she believed what Florence told her—that these people never bathed. There was little evidence of labor. Idle men and women smoking cigarettes lolled about, some silent, others jabbering. They did not resent the visit of the American women, nor did they show hospitality. They appeared stupid. Disease was rampant in these houses; when the doors were shut there was no ventilation, and even with the doors open Madeline felt choked and stifled. A powerful penetrating odor pervaded the rooms that were less stifling then others, and this odor Florence explained came from a liquor the Mexicans distilled from a cactus plant. Here drunkenness was manifest, a terrible inert drunkenness that made its victims deathlike.[5]

Whether the negative traits were caused by the obvious poverty, or vice-versa, was a question Grey indirectly addressed. He created a situation where Majesty, the wealthy eastern woman, puts the Mexicans to work cleaning their village. This injection of money changes the appearance of the village, but does not change the Mestizos' propensity for drink, gambling, and violence.

According to Grey's social commentary, Mexicans were cursed with highly emotional natures, and were susceptible to vice, a common Anglo stereotype of lower-class Mexicans. Grey ran no risk in antagonizing his readers when he included it in his description of Arizona's extreme southern reaches.

Much of Grey's dislike for Mexicans, whether upper or lower class, stemmed from the program of extermination the Mexican government used toward the Yaqui Indians. Forced Yaqui enslavement on the Yucatán henequen (agave) plantations ended in 1910, just two years prior to Grey's initial visit, and the Yaquis were returned to their homeland in Sonora, with an intense hatred of the Mexicans. Grey made use of the Yaqui's story in the novel *Desert Gold* and in a short story, "Yaqui."

In *Desert Gold*, the entire tribe's situation is personified in the character, appropriately named "Yaqui." His background is outlined in order to dramatize the actions of the Mexican government.

> I got some of his story and guessed the rest. The Mexican government is trying to root out the Yaquis. A year ago his tribe was taken in chains to a Mexican port on the Gulf. The fathers, mothers, children were separated and put in ships bound for Yucatán. There they were made slaves on the great henequen plantations. They were driven, beaten, starved. Each slave had for a day's rations a hunk of sourdough, no more. Yucatán is low, marshy, damp, hot. The Yaquis were bred on the high, dry Sonoran plateau where the air is like a knife. They dropped dead in the henequen fields and their places were taken by more. You see, the Mexicans won't kill outright in their war of extermination of the Yaquis. They get use out of them.[6]

Passages such as this make Grey's sympathies very clear. In his eyes, the Mexican government was guilty of unspeakable atrocities toward Yaquis, yet more evidence of their cruelty and arrogance.

Grey sympathized with the Yaquis, extolled their virtues, and spared no pity for the Mexican government, but did not credit the Yaquis with meekness. The theme of brutal Yaqui revenge is woven into the story, leading to a dramatic scene in which the Yaqui force a Mexican over a cliff, where he is impaled on cholla spines, and dies an agonizing and protracted death.

The theme of Yaqui revenge is also given a prominent place in the short story, "Yaqui." This story opens in the Sonoran desert, where a band of Indians is fleeing west, away from the Mexicans. The main character, Yaqui, is the leader of the group. The band is captured and shipped to Yucatán, and Yaqui is separated from his wife and infant son. He is worked unmercifully, but develops a talent for operating the iron press that makes henequen bales. It is through his skill with the press that he gains his revenge by killing the man who had separated him from his family. Half of the story involves the flight from the Mexicans on the Sonoran desert, and the other half, slavery in the Yucatán; it is the theme, plot, and characters rather than the setting that groups this short story with the southern Arizona pieces. The Yaqui's stoic endurance of suffering, his nobility, and the intricate and hideous revenge that he planned, expand upon themes introduced in *Desert Gold*. Because the story focuses upon the Yaqui's tragedy rather than treating it as a peripheral issue, more of the history of the war between the Yaquis and the Mexicans is included, and Mexican cruelty is highlighted.

One reason for Grey's unconditional sympathy for the Yaquis was his belief that they were direct descendants of the Aztecs. Although this assumption may make anthropologists shudder and fails to take into account any number of other native groupings related to the Aztecs, Grey used it to explain the antipathy between Mexican and Yaqui.

> As for hard sights—wait till you've seen a Yaqui do up a Mexican. Bar none, that is the limit! It's blood lust, a racial hate deep as life and terrible. The Spaniards crushed the Aztecs four or five hundred years ago. That hate has had time to grow as deep as a cactus root. The Yaquis are mountain Aztecs.[7]

Grey's racial theories were at least consistent, if not particularly accurate. He saw nobility and other virtues in the so-called pure races, such as Spanish or Yaqui, but felt that racial mixture produced corruption and degeneration. His theories and opinions on that topic were in tune with the times, but reveal an interesting contradiction when compared with his attitudes toward the intermixture of the American Indian and the Anglo as revealed in *The Vanishing American*, in which he advocates such a mixture to save the Indian from doom. Grey's ideas on race were founded on the firm belief in Anglo superiority, typical of his time. Any mixture of races in which the Caucasian group was part resulted in the overpowering of the inferior race, while a mixture of any other two races produced only decay. Uncorrupted races, such as the Yaqui, could retain their virtue and vitality if unmolested by others.

Along with consideration of Mexicans and Yaquis, Grey's southern Arizona novels address the role of Anglos who lived along the border. Most of the main characters in the books are Anglos, and almost all of them are involved in cattle ranching in one way or another. The lonely outpost in *Desert Gold* is a cattle ranch, and the ranch developed by Majesty Hammond in *The Light of Western Stars* is a working ranch with numerous cowboys. *Majesty's Rancho,* published in 1937, continues the saga of Majesty Hammond's ranch, focusing on her daughter, a liberated young college woman named Madge. The ranch encounters increasing problems with government interference, decreasing range land, and competition from Argentine beef importation. Further cattle rustling is complicated by gangsters and bootleggers. The financial crisis of the thirties throws the ranch on hard times, which are compounded by Madge's uncontrolled spending.

Descriptions of cattle ranching in all three novels are vivid. Too, the inclusion of numerous cowboys in these stories gives Grey the opportunity to utilize them in dramatic or humorous situations.

One of the more interesting of the cowboy characters is Monty Price. He appears in *The Light of Western Stars* as a "very short, wizened little man, ludicrously bowlegged, with a face the color and hardness of a burned-out cinder."[8] Price's physical disabilities stem from his rescue of a child from a forest fire in the Tonto Basin. The rescue itself is a plot of one of Grey's finest short stories, "Monty Price's Nightingale." In this story, after the heroic rescue, Price drifts to a ranch on the southern border, where his injuries prevent him from doing much real work, but where he is loved. Grey retrieves the character from the short story and includes him in the novel, giving him more depth in the process. In the novel, however, Price is a gunman as well as a cowboy; he has roamed the ranges from Missouri to Montana, and his injuries surely must have healed, as Grey has him participating in the round-up quite effectively. Price meets his end in a gunfight defending Majesty's reputation. This character is more developed than other fictional cowboys in the southern Arizona novels. For the most part, they simply serve the purpose of providing background, humor, and a western flavor to Grey's stories.

In Grey's novels, cowboys outnumber prospectors, but Grey was nonetheless interested in the motives of the men who turned their backs on civilization and spent lonely months or even years on the desert, searching for that elusive gleam of ore. Once again, the effect of the desert environment captivated Grey. Two short stories concentrate on prospectors, who were later incorporated into full-length novels.

After his first trip to the southern deserts, Grey wrote a short story entitled "Fantoms of Peace." This story is set in Death Valley, and involves a strange friendship that develops between two men who come to the desert for different reasons: one to remember, the other to forget. An interesting sidelight of the tale is Grey's description of waterwitching, but the main theme is that of compassion for others and forgiveness. The same story is moved to the "wild border line between Sonora and Arizona," and used, with very few changes, as the prologue in *Desert Gold*. The two prospectors become Nell Warren's father and grandfather, each of whom has wronged her mother, and provide some of the background and plot twists for the love story between Nell and the main character, Richard Gale.

Much later, Grey wrote another short story about prospectors, which is also set in extreme southern Arizona. Entitled "Amber's Mirage" (1929), it once again examines the relationship between two men who are alone on the desert. In this story, an older prospector takes a younger man with him into the desert, with the motive of saving him from a girl who, he judges, would break his heart. The younger man is induced to go along by visions of fabulous wealth that would impress the girl. The two become lost in the desert, and the older one dies with a peculiar mirage before his eyes. The mirage is only a reflection of the sunset, but it remains imprinted on the lifeless eyes. Although the older man urges the other to leave him and save himself, the younger refuses to go, an iteration of Grey's theme of loyalty, compassion for others, and selflessness. The younger man survives the desert and returns to the girl with his "bucket of gold," only to find she has married another in his absence. Brokenhearted, he flees to the desert, where he finds peace.

These two stories present the type of Anglo Grey imagined in the southern Arizona deserts. They explore the motives of men, their relationship to each other, and allow the dramatization of such universal themes as loyalty, guilt, forgiveness, sacrifice, and selflessness.

The desert captivated Grey, and he attempted to describe the fascination it held for him in an article entitled "What the Desert Means to Me."

The desert, of course, has been most compelling and most il-
luminating to me. The lure of the silent waste places of the earth,
how inexplicable and tremendous! Why do men sacrifice love,
home, civilization for the solitude of the lonely land? How in-
finite the fascination of death and decay and desolation—the secret of the desert.[9]

Paramount in his contemplation was an assessment of the effect it had on
people who were isolated on it for protracted lengths of time. California's Death Valley and the Sonoran Desert of northern Mexico and
southern Arizona particulary interested him.

Grey wrote that the desert has two important effects: One is the
human tendency to regress to the savage, and the other is the desert's
power to magnify human characteristics, whether good or bad. Grey
considered the retrogression of civilized human beings to the savage on
the desert in several novels and short stories. His attitudes toward this
aspect varied, however. Sometimes this retrogression is described in a
positive fashion, as a way of avoiding insanity or as a means of survival.
Stranger from the Tonto, set in the Sonoran Desert, provides a good example of this.

Lastly, he cautioned Kent against the insidious encroachment of
the desert upon a man's sanity. If he gave himself over to the un-
thinking sensorial perceptions of the savage he could survive.
But to think and brood and grieve would be fatal.[10]

At other times, this reaction is portrayed as dangerous, in itself leading
to insanity. From *Desert Gold:*

He had trained himself, in order to fight a paralyzing something
in the deserts' influence, to oppose with memory and thought an
insidious primitive retrogression to what was scarcely consciousness at all, merely a savage's instinct of sight and sound.[11]

Regardless, he asserted that a return to the primitive was an inevitable
result.

Grey pondered why the desert had this apparent effect on people. Although he never really reached a satisfactory conclusion, he suggested
that this characteristic was linked with whatever made the desert allur-
ing. In "What the Desert Means to Me," he explains that

in every man and woman there survives the red blood of our ancestors, the primitive instincts. In these hides the secret of the
eloquent and tremendous influence of the desert. The wide, open
spaces, the lonely hills, the desolate rocky wastes, the shifting
sands and painted steppes, the stark naked canyons—all these
places of the desert with their loneliness and silence and solitude
awake the instincts of the primitive age of man.[12]

A bit further into the article, Grey made his point more bluntly: "Men do
not love the forbidding and desolate desert for the reasons that they
imagine, but because of the ineradicable and unconscious wildness of
savage nature in them." The primitive desert appealed to something
equally as elemental concealed under a layer of civilization, and given
time, exposed it. The desert had this power because

'the desert is like the Earth in the beginning,' replied the old
prospector sagely. 'After awhile it takes a man back to what he
was when he first evolved from some lower organism. He gets
closer to the origin of life an' the end of life.'[13]

Grey thought that the desert's similarity to primal memories of environment created a situation wherein people reverted to a more primitive
consciousness. Its loneliness and solitude, its forced confrontation with
the elements, and its grim reminders of an ever-present death aroused
savage emotions.

These same features created the other effect of the desert that fascinated Grey, its tendency to reveal and magnify a man's nature. Grey
commented that Death Valley was "a place to face one's soul." This
was, according to him, characteristic of deserts in general.

After a few weeks in the desert he had always become a different
man. In civilization, in the rough mining camps, he had been a
prey to unrest and gloom; but once down on the great heave and
bulge and sweep of this lonely world, he could look into his un-
quiet soul without bitterness. Always he began to see and to
think and to feel. Did not the desert magnify men? Cameron believed that wild men in wild places, fighting cold, heat, starvation, thirst, barrenness, facing the elements in all their primal
ferocity, usually retrograded, descended to the savage, lost all

heart and soul, and became mere brutes. Likewise he believed
that men lost in the wilderness often reversed that brutal order of
life, and became noble, wonderful, superhuman.[14]

In the desert, according to Grey, men behaved as their characters dic-
tated: if they were inherently good, their goodness was magnified; if
they were naturally evil, they became downright savage. Thus, the desert was a stage for dramas concerning the nature of humankind, and the
southern Arizona deserts afforded Grey the opportunity to incorporate
this into his writing.

Oddly, the settings and the characters Grey described in his southern
Arizona tales were at variance with the reality of the region. His settings
consisted of only isolated desert areas along the extreme southern border, never the populous cities of Tucson or Phoenix, and despite the colorful history of Tombstone, located in the state's southeastern corner,
that city never appeared in his novels or stories. While he wrote of
"pure-blooded" Spanish ladies, there were actually no aristocratic Spanish families in southern Arizona at the time Grey visited there, and his
descriptions of the Mexicans were highly prejudiced. His southern deserts were populated with prospectors, but he wrote no novels which featured miners, important individuals in southern Arizona, both then and
now. This wide gap between the reality of the southern deserts and
Grey's descriptions of the region was the result of the relatively few
visits Grey actually made there.

Grey's experiences in the borderlands of Arizona produced three
novels and four short stories. When compared with the literary output
associated with some of the other Arizona locales, this seems meager,
yet the southern Arizona novels stand apart from the rest. They incorporate the Spanish and Mexican heritage of the Southwest, and explore the
international rivalries of the United States with its neighbor to the south.
To a greater degree than any of the other works based in Arizona, they
speak of the effect of the environment on humanity, the thesis of Grey's
perception of the West. Grey carried his interest in this theme into his
writings associated with the fourth and final area, the Tonto Basin and
the Mogollon Rim.

CHAPTER VIII

TALES OF THE
TONTO

Arizona's wild Tonto Basin attracted Zane Grey's interest when he went there in 1915 with his old friend and guide, Al Doyle. This was a hunting excursion in the White Mountains, but Grey found more there than just recreation. He found a land with an intriguing history, a setting that stirred his imagination, and people who impressed him with their hard lives and rustic simplicity. Grey returned to the Tonto Basin and the Mogollon Rim eleven times over the following fourteen years, and in 1920 purchased three acres just under the rim for a hunting lodge. With few exceptions, he spent each autumn at his lodge, hunting in the Tonto Basin and writing. He was rewarded with settings, plots, characters and themes for his books, and his literary output associated with the Tonto was greater than that associated with any other region of Arizona. Fourteen romances and twelve short stories and nonfictional articles were the products of Grey's infatuation with the region. These explored several rim-country episodes: feuds, outlaws and gunmen, cattle ranching and cowboys, pioneer experiences, and the land itself.

Grey's excitement was provoked by the Tonto Basin's Pleasant Valley War, and he spent part of his 1918 trip to the area searching for information concerning this feud. He explains in the foreword of *To the*

Last Man that it was not until his third trip in search of material in 1920 that he broke through the residents' reluctance to talk and was able to gather any information, and was then swamped with accounts of the feud, many of them contradictory. Grey attributed his version to two people.

> Best of all I ran across an old Tonto Basin man, pioneer, named Elan Boles. He went through the Pleasant Valley War and told us the story. It is a wonderful thing. The war really and truly was not between sheep men + cattle men, but between rustlers + honest ranchers.
>
> A good many men want to tell us the story, so we hear, for obvious reasons. But I'm glad Boles got to me first.[1]

In a short story entitled "The Secret of Quaking-Asp Cabin" (1924), he attributes the tale to a Matthew Taylor, characterized as a Mormon pioneer. Grey utilized numerous sources in his quest for material about the feud and searched diligently for details of the episode, but what appears in his novel *To the Last Man* is a romance loosely twined around a factual framework, rather than a precise and accurate history.

The central theme of *To the Last Man* is a romance between Jean Isbel, a cattleman, and Ellen Jorth, an associate of sheepmen and rustlers. In the novel, the conflict's roots lay in Texas, where the patriarch of the Isbels and the leader of the Jorths love the same woman. The two families find their way to Arizona, where the feud erupts, disguised as a sheepmen-versus-cattlemen conflict, but is complicated by the involvement of a gang of Texas cattle rustlers known as the Hashknife outfit. The Hashknife gang, led by a Texan named Daggs, is associated with the Jorth faction.

There is a thread of historical authenticity in this novel. There was a minor rivalry on that range, rustling had occurred, and employees of the Aztec Land and Cattle Company, known locally as the Hashknife outfit, were involved in the feud.[2] The romance between two members of the rival factions, the roots of the feud in the leaders' love for the same woman, and the importance of the sheep and cattle rivalry were, however, entirely fictionalized.

Grey's acquaintance with the Hashknife outfit came through his study of the Graham-Tewksbury feud and led him to write a romance that chronicled the outfit's last days. The outfit was assembled when the

Atchison, Topeka and Santa Fe Railroad formed the Aztec Land and Cattle Company with a group of Texas cattlemen.[3] In order to squeeze their competition and gain a large amount of land, the Santa Fe forced the financially desperate Atlantic and Pacific Railroad to sell to the Aztec Company over a million acres of land in northern Arizona at a loss. They then imported cattle, and hired a gang of Texas cowboys to stand guard over the land. The Texan cowboys gained a reputation for harassing both the Mormon settlers, who had homesteaded in the area beginning in 1871, and the sheepherders, who grazed their flocks on land claimed by the Aztec Company.[4] John Paine, hired to drive off sheepmen, fled to Pleasant Valley with eight others when Winslow vigilantes tired of their activities and joined the Graham faction.[5]

Grey's novelization of the Hashknife cowboys is set seven years after the Pleasant Valley episode. In the novel, appropriately entitled *The Hash Knife Outfit* (1933), Grey dramatizes the band's disintegration and demise. According to the novel, the Hashknife was not always on the wrong side of the law, but became associated with a few outlaws that gave the entire outfit a bad name. As one of the characters explains:

Men, I rode on the first Hash Knife Outfit, twenty years ago . . . an' Arizona never had a finer bunch of riders. Since then I've rode in all the outfits. Some had good men an' bad men at the same time. Thet Texas outfit in the early 'eighties gave the Hash Knife its bad name. Daggs, Colter, an' the rest didn't live long, but their fame did. Yet they wasn't any worse then the cattlemen and sheepmen who fought that war.[6]

Although the disintegration of the Hashknife is dramatized in the book and is not blamed on the veteran cowboys, this serves only as a backdrop for the dual romances between Jim Traft and Molly Dunn, and Jim's tenderfoot sister, Gloriana, and Curly, one of the cowboys. Few solid historical facts are included in the novel, but Grey's interest in the Hashknife, as well as his sense of what would thrill his readers, prompted him to refer to it in at least five more of the Tonto Basin books: *Nevada, 30,000 on the Hoof, Shadow on the Trail, Stranger from the Tonto,* and *The Drift Fence.*

Directly related to Grey's interest in famous feuds and range wars of the Southwest was his intrigue with the gunfighter.[7] Several Tonto Basin tales feature the gunman as the main character, and Grey's characterization develops him as a stock figure used later in western novels and films. These stories are not based upon actual historical events or characters, but have been created for the purpose of enhancing the stereotypical figure of the western gunfighter.

The most popular gunman of the Tonto Basin books is found in the novel *Nevada*. First published in 1926, this book is a sequel to *Forlorn River* and titled for the main character, whose real name is Jim Lacy. In *Forlorn River,* Nevada befriends Ben Ide and saves him from disgrace and doom. In so doing, he falls in love with Ben's sister, Hettie, who reforms him; eventually he is forced to flee from the area—leaving his friend and Hettie behind—because, to save Ben, he has killed a man. *Nevada* opens with Jim Lacy escaping across the Sierra Nevada. He ultimately drifts into the Tonto Basin of Arizona; unbeknown to him, the Ides have sold their California ranch and moved to Arizona in search of their friend. The new ranch is plagued with rustlers, and Lacy, who keeps his identity a secret and avoids the Ides, tries to discover the thieves' identities and end their activities.

Jim "Nevada" Lacy has a dark and lurid past, but is in truth a noble character, saved by the love of a woman; he values loyalty, friendship, and honor. An almost chivalrous figure, he defends the honor of women, even the dance hall girls. Self-sacrifice for the welfare of his friends is his motivating force, and he uses his gun only when necessary. As a gunfighter, he is not a sinister outlaw, but a lone figure of justice.

Wade Holden, the gunman and reformed outlaw in *Shadow on the Trail,* is similar to Jim "Nevada" Lacy. In his flight from the Texas Rangers, Holden is hidden and protected by a young woman. After drifting about Arizona and New Mexico, Holden encounters her again in the Tonto Basin, where her family has established a cattle ranch regularly visited by rustlers. Holden, like Lacy, repays his debt by chasing the rustlers off the range. Like Nevada, Holden is loyal to his friends, repays his debts, and defends helpless and unfortunate women.

A slightly different type of gunman appears as the main character in *Arizona Ames*. Richard Ames becomes a drifting cowboy and do-gooder after killing a man in defense of his twin sister. Everywhere he wanders, he becomes involved in his friends' problems and uses his gun to rescue them. Ames differs from the previously discussed gunmen in two ways. First, his family background and the forces that lead him to a gunslinger's life are delineated, while both Lacy and Holden are homeless men. Secondly, Ames is first a cowboy rather than a gunman, but circumstances give him a reputation for gunplay. Both Nevada and Holden later adopt the protective coloration of the ranch hand, but Arizona Ames is a reluctant gunman with a family left behind in the Tonto. This insight into the character gives him more depth than either Lacy or Holden.

The character of the gunfighter is developed in *Arizona Clan*. Set in the Tonto Basin, the story features Dodge Mercer, who wanders into the Tonto, meets Nan Lilley and her family, and decides to help them with their problems. When asked about his nickname, Mercer responds:

> Back on the plains I earned that name. . . . I never dodged trouble in all the ten years I rode the range. I never dodged a night's watch, or a stampede of stock, or a rustling outfit, or cards, or gamblers, or women, or fights, or bullets—nor dealing death. That's why they called me Dodge. I rode away at last because I wanted to dodge all those damned things—to find a new life among new faces where there wasn't any trouble. But I guess there's no such place on earth. I rode a thousand miles or more to run into you and your trouble—which I shall make mine.[8]

Dodge evidently has had a wild past like Nevada and Holden, and is attempting to escape his reputation. Like Richard Ames, he becomes a western knight errant who adopts and solves the problems of other people. The character of Dodge Mercer is a composite of Grey's earlier fictional gunmen; he has Lacy's and Holden's unsavory past and Ames's penchant for doing good.

The gunfighter character, with variations, is the main figure in *Stranger from the Tonto*. Although the action in this novel does not take place in the Tonto Basin, much is made of the fact that Kent Wingfield is from the Tonto. Additionally, he cultivates the rumor that he had been one of the Hashknife Outfit and had participated in the Drift Fence War and the Yellow Jacket Feud, veiled references to the Pleasant Valley War.[9] The only real reference to Wingfield's past, other than being from the Tonto, is in the opening chapter of the book where his association with an old prospector is discussed. This prospector, himself a reformed outlaw, reveals to Wingfield the location of Hole-in-the-Rock, a robber's hideout in southern Utah, and sends him on a quest to rescue the robber's daughter. Wingfield is the only one of Grey's gunmen who has any connection with prospecting.

The Tonto gunfighter is also the subject of one of Grey's short stories, "The Saga of the Ice-Cream Kid."[10] This story involves a young outlaw who is rescued from death on the desert by a cattle outfit. The Kid, as he is called, proves to be a likable young man who is reformed by the company of the cowboys, while his companion, Coyote McKee, continues his evil ways. When McKee lures the rancher's son, a friend of the Kid, toward a life of crime, the Kid responds by goading McKee into a duel. He shoots McKee while nonchalantly eating ice cream, a feat that earns him the sobriquet of "The Ice-Cream Kid." Again, the gunman is a rootless individual without a past who has fallen into crime, but reforms. Forced to resort to violence to protect his friends, he proves his loyalty and basic trustworthiness. Even in the short story form, Grey's gunfighter follows the basic pattern established in *Nevada, Forlorn River, Shadow on the Trail, Arizona Ames, Stranger from the Tonto,* and *Arizona Clan.*

Grey's most interesting characterization of the gunfighter is his treatment of William Bonney, alias Billy the Kid, in *Shadow on the Trail.*

> Wade met and felt the clearest coldest eyes that it had ever been his fortune to gaze into. They seemed to search his very soul. Billy the Kid was not unprepossessing. But for a prominent tooth, which he exposed when he laughed, he would have been almost handsome. It was a smooth, reckless, youthful face, singularly cold, as if carved out of stone. Wade's divination here recognized the spirit of the wildness of the West at its height. Billy the Kid was what the West had made him. He looked a boy, he had the freshness of a boy, but he was a man, and one in whom fear had never been born.[11]

Billy the Kid, according to Grey, was the epitome of the lawless West, and a product of the land. He reacted to his environment by becoming as wild, ungovernable, and ruthless as it was. Like Grey's other fictional gunfighters, Billy the Kid is a man with a dim past but capable of great loyalty to his friends; he leaps to their defense or to avenge transgressions against them. According to Grey, Billy the Kid's participation in the Lincoln County War is precipitated by the murder of an English rancher who was his friend. This account, however brief, is accurate, as William Bonney (whose given name was Henry McCarty) is actually pulled into the Lincoln County conflict between John Chisum, Alexander McSween, and Englishman John Tunstall, all of whom were locked in a feud with the L. G. Murphy company and their henchmen. Tunstall, Billy's employer, is killed by Murphy's men. Historically, the Kid's notorious career of banditry is said to have begun when he meted out justice to those who had killed his employer and friend. While Grey acknowledged that he was a violent and dangerous man, he instilled his fictional portrayal of him with the same loyalty that he attributed to his entirely fictional gunmen.

All of these gunmen symbolized Grey's idea that the most important, and cruelest, lesson taught by the West was that of self-preservation. On the frontier, Grey thought, survival depended upon the ability to defend oneself. Grey's knightly gunslingers did so with deadly expertise and efficiency.

The frontier cattle industry also served as a backdrop for a number of Grey's Tonto romances. In these novels and short stories, Grey was most concerned with portraying the life and the character of the men associated most closely with cattle ranching, the cowboys. He also dealt with the bane of the western rancher's life, rustlers, and in one poignant novel he dramatized the life of the rancher's wife. Each of the Tonto Basin cattle tales, despite their specific emphasis, celebrate the demanding and formative nature of the environment, the beauty of the Tonto Basin setting, and the wildness and lawlessness of the land.

Drift Fence is the first Tonto book written by Grey that concentrates on the cattle industry. Vintage 1929, it is the story of young Jim Traft who comes west to learn the cattle business on his uncle's Tonto Basin ranch. His uncle wants Jim to learn the task of running a large cattle ranch because he has named Jim his heir. The young man's first responsibility is the construction of a drift fence in order to control his grazing, wandering cattle. Jim's uncle gives him a construction crew that is one of the ranch's rowdiest outfits. The bulk of the novel consists of Jim's trials in building the fence and controlling his workers.

Each of Jim's problems presents a challenge, which when conquered, results in another successful adaptation to the West. The cowboys resent the presence of the owner's nephew as their boss, and go out of their way to make life miserable for him. Curly, Bud, and Lonestar play the inevitable good-humored cowboy tricks on him, but one of the men, Hack Jocelyn, is blatantly antagonistic. Neighboring ranchers and homesteaders do not want the fence to go up, and try to sabotage its construction. Finally, young Traft falls in love with Molly, a homesteader's daughter whose gunfighting brother hates him. By the end of the book,

Jim establishes himself with the cowboys, proves his worth to his uncle, completes the most difficult section of the fence, learns the ways of the West, and wins the love of the girl and the friendship of her brother. Jim Traft's trials in *Drift Fence* harden him into a courageous, resourceful westerner.

Grey's trademark theme is further developed in *The Dude Ranger* (1930). The main character, Ernest Selby, resembles Grey's characters in *Drift Fence* and *The Hash Knife Outfit* in that he, too, comes to the West to assume ownership of a ranch in Arizona. Selby's Red Rock Ranch is bequeathed to him by his uncle and has been managed by a man named Hepford. During the preceding three years, the ranch had suffered a serious loss of stock, and in order to discover the cause, Selby decides to pass himself as a cowboy, rather than declare his status as the owner. Unfortunately, he proves to be a raw greenhorn who cannot stay on a horse, and becomes the object of scorn and derision, often falling victim to cowboy pranks. Despite numerous setbacks, he continues with his efforts to become a real westerner. At the conclusion of the novel, Selby reveals his true identity and discloses the dishonesty of the ranch manager; he does not press charges, though, as he has married the man's daughter. More importantly, he has established himself in the eyes of the cowboys, has been accepted by them, and has developed the qualities needed for survival and success in the West.[12]

The problem of rustling is a central theme in several of the Tonto Basin books. *Shadow on the Trail* and *Sunset Pass* deal directly with the subject of cattle theft. The theme is addressed as well in *The Hash Knife Outfit* and *The Dude Ranger,* although it is not the central theme of either novel. In highlighting this particular problem, Grey reflected the very real concerns of the western cattle industry.

Sunset Pass (1927), also addresses the issue of cattle theft, but demonstrates a slightly different mode. Although the novel is set in western New Mexico, somewhere in the vicinity of Deming, it is actually an Arizona tale. (The story was first told to Grey by Lee Doyle, who claimed that the original Sunset Pass was in the Mogollon Mountains south of Winslow.)[13] In this book, the main character, Trueman Rock, returns to the town of Wagontongue after a six-year absence motivated by his killing of a man in a duel. Upon his return, he meets Thiry Preston and promptly falls in love with her. He follows the girl to her family's ranch in Sunset Pass and is hired by her father as a cowboy.

Strange rumors seem to follow the Prestons, and area ranchers begin to suspect they are cattle thieves. It is Trueman Rock who finally discovers that Thiry's father and brother are indeed stealing cattle, butchering them, hiding the heads and hides, and shipping the meat to wholesalers in other parts. Instead of driving herds of stolen cattle to the nearest train station, the Preston men dispose of the evidence—the hide with the brand and the head with the earmark—and transport the marketable parts of the beef to the nearest purchaser. Because the evidence is so well hidden, and there are no large cattle movements, proof of the rustling is difficult to produce.

In addition to dealing with a unique type of cattle theft, *Sunset Pass* stands apart from Grey's other novels in another, very different way. Thiry Preston is unusually close to her brother Ash; indeed she seems to be completely under his control. Several incidents hint at a relationship that goes beyond the usual affection between brother and sister, and the brother's irrational jealousy, suspicion, and possessiveness make one suspect that Grey has introduced the theme of incest into this novel. One passage of the novel amplifies this thought:

> Ash wrapped his long arms around her, and hugging her closely, he bent his head over her. The action seemed eloquent, beautiful, and yet it carried a hint of bold raw nature. . . . But Rock's heat and rancor lost itself in something worse—jealousy. It had seared him to see Thiry run to Ash, almost with arms outstretched, her face flushed, her eyes alight, her voice broken, to receive that strange caress.[14]

At the conclusion of the novel Trueman Rock must fight Ash and kill him, thus risking the loss of Thiry's love. After Ash is dead, Thiry's father reveals that Ash is not her real brother, but a foundling he had rescued and adopted. While the spectre of incest is nicely laid to rest, the explanation does not quite account for the emotion Thiry felt while she was under the impression that Ash was her brother. This hint of incest makes the novel unusual among Grey's other western romances.

Another atypical western is *30,000 on the Hoof*. Published in 1940, it was originally entitled *The Frontier Wife*. The title was changed because the publishers felt it did not have quite the western flavor associated with the Zane Grey name.[15] Unusual in that it is written from a woman's point of view, it chronicles a Tonto Basin ranch wife.

The storyline is based, at least in part, upon an actual person, a young scout from General Crook's army who homesteads a valley near the Mogollon Rim and establishes a cattle ranch there. The rest of the book is a fictional account of the problems he faces in his attempts to accumulate thirty thousand head of cattle.

The protagonist, Logan Huett, invites his childhood friend, Lucinda Baker, to join him at the homestead. Although the young woman had not seen him for a number of years, she agrees. The couple encounters every imaginable obstacle to success: weather, predatory animals, loneliness, injuries, insects, crows, and even rustlers. At one point, Lucinda is raped by a renegade Apache, and the second of her three sons is evidently half-Apache.[16] An abandoned baby girl, found near the Huett ranch, is later added to the family. The issue of incest appears once again, as the daughter matures and develops a close relationship with her half-breed brother. When it is revealed that she is not a blood relative, they marry. Finally, after many years of ranching, it appears that Lucinda and Logan will reach their goal of owning thirty thousand head.

The story's conclusion is particularly poignant. As the United States enters World War I and hysteria sweeps the nation, Logan and Lucinda sell their cattle to the government. This is followed by a series of disasters: the government agent swindles them out of their money, all three sons are killed in the war, their daughter goes insane, and Logan becomes senile. Only Lucinda's strength remains.

30,000 on the Hoof stands apart from Grey's other western novels by virtue of its harsh presentation of life. It does not address idealized situations or people, but is instead an effort at realism. A chronicle of a couple's struggle to establish a life in the West, this novel also shows Grey's ability to write with rare insight into the soul of a strong woman. This departure from his typical style presents a far more realistic view of life in the West, and many critics consider this to be one of the best books Grey produced.

Just as the books about the cattle industry applaud qualities developed by range life, Grey's stories about homesteading and hunting in the Tonto Basin and on the Mogollon Rim praise characteristics molded by that rugged life, and celebrate the exhilaration of the hunt. In 1919, Zane Grey made the acquaintance of the Haught family, rim country pioneers. In the company of the clan's patriarch, A. L. "Babe" Haught, and his sons Edd and Richard, Grey hunted bear, deer, and turkey, and it was from the Haughts that Grey purchased three acres of land for his own hunting lodge.

Two books directly based on the Haught family, *Code of the West* and *Under the Tonto Rim*, utilize a traditional Grey plot. In the former, published in 1934, Georgianna May is sent west to join her sister Lucy Stockwell—a Tonto Basin schoolteacher—to be cured "of a slight tendency toward tuberculosis, and a very great leaning toward indiscriminate flirtation."[17] A modern 1920s flapper, Georgianna wears her skirts too short, bobs her hair, paints her face, and wreaks havoc among the young men of the three Thurman families with whom she and Lucy board. In short, she thoroughly shocks the entire countryside. Pushing modern manners too far for the little country community, she accepts a marriage proposal from the youngest of the Thurman boys. All the neighbors, including her new relatives, think her to be a somewhat less than desirable addition to the family. She realizes that "what might be done with impunity back in the sophisticated East could not be done at all here in the Tonto."[18] The simple western values reveal the loss of morality of the East, yet Georgianna's exposure to the West reforms her. Imbued with its qualities, she is able to vindicate herself, convince her husband of her virtue, redeem her soiled reputation, and win the respect of the community.

In this novel, the Thurman clan is modeled after the Haught family. Grey describes the Thurmans and reflects the "Code of the West," in the following glowing way:

> During her years teaching in the Tonto, Miss Stockwell had never seen a Thurman, or any of their relatives under the influence of liquor. They did not lie. If they made a promise it would be kept. Clean, fine, virile, manly young giants they all seemed to her. They smoked cigarettes, of their own making, and they would fight at the drop of a sombrero. They were cool, easy, tranquil, contented young backwoodsmen, strong and resourceful in the open, full of a latent fire and reserve force seldom called upon. They loved jokes, tricks, and dances.[19]

This passage reveals not only Grey's opinion of the Haughts, but his ideal of the western man as well.

Under the Tonto Rim (1925), is even more directly based upon the Haught clan. In this novel, Edd Haught appears as Edd Denmeade, and Myrtle Haught, one of the Haught's daughters, appears as Mertie Denmeade.[20] The story centers upon the character of Lucy Watson, a young welfare worker in the Tonto area, and her sister Clara. The real hero of the story, however, is Edd Denmeade. His woodsmanship, prowess, courage, and honor are portrayed through a number of episodes. At the conclusion of the story, the backwoods farmer Edd wins the city girl Lucy for a wife. In the process, the reader is introduced to the Tonto Basin way of life, bee hunting, a wild western dance, and the effects of white mule, Tonto Basin moonshine whiskey.

Whiskey plays a more prominent role in the novel *Arizona Clan*. This book, published in 1950, is based on settler life in the Tonto. In this story, ex-gunslinger Dodge Mercer drifts to the Tonto and encounters the Lilley family, homesteaders down on their luck. Their main product, sorghum, was the principal ingredient of white mule. The father of the Lilley clan is dying due to the effects of homemade alcohol on his health, while the sons are involved in drinking white mule and even aiding in thefts from their father's farm. Buck Hathaway, the villain of the piece, masterminds the thefts of sorghum, produces the drink, and plies the family with it. As a result, he gains powerful control over the Lilleys and schemes to take over their ranch and marry the daughter, Nan. Dodge Mercer, however, falls in love with Nan and undertakes the defense of both her and her family.

Man of the Forest explores life in the Tonto Basin from a unique viewpoint. This novel's main character is Milt Dale, who lives at the base of Old Baldy, highest of the White Mountain peaks, rising to over ten thousand feet. Grey's geography is accurate, as he evidently locates his character's home near Baldy Peak, which at 11,590 feet is the tallest point of the White Mountain ridge near McNary and Springerville. Milt Dale had run away from home at fourteen and tried a number of different occupations, none of which suited him. At thirty years old, he resides on the mountain by himself, as he does not care for human society, and accumulates animal companions instead. Occasionally he ventures down into town, where he has a few friends, but his uncouth appearance, aloofness, and propensity for bringing his pet mountain lion with him make him unwelcome in most establishments. His solitude is disturbed when he overhears a plot to kidnap Helen Rayner, a young woman who is coming west to join her uncle, and hold her hostage while forcing concessions from her wealthy and powerful relative. Unable to convince the uncle of the danger, Milt Dale rides to Helen's defense, taking her to his mountain hideaway until all danger has passed. While there, the two fall in love.

This was one of Grey's earliest Tonto Basin novels, written in 1917, and Grey endows the region with all the symbolic meaning that it had for him. In it, he discusses several topics that were significant to him personally, including religion and nature, self-preservation, survival of the fittest, the balance of nature, and reason versus instinct.

Religion is discussed from the viewpoint of the man of the woods, Milt Dale.

> Maybe I have a religion. I don't know. But its not the kind you have—not the Bible kind. That kind doesn't keep men in Pine and Snowdrop an' all over—sheepmen an' ranchers an' farmers an' travelers, such as I've known—the religion they profess doesn't keep them from lyin', cheatin', stealin', and killin'. I reckon no man lives as I do—which perhaps is my religion—will lie or cheat or steal or kill, unless its to kill in self-defense. . . . My religion, maybe, is love of life—wild life as it was in the beginning—an' the wind that blows secrets from everywhere, an' the water that sings all day an' all night, an' the stars that shine constant, an' the trees that speak somehow, an' the rocks that aren't dead. I'm never alone here or on the trails. There's somethin' unseen, but always with me. An' that's It! Call it God if you like.[21]

As he did in the novels centered on the Indian reservations and those dealing with Mormonism, Grey indicts organized religion for its shallowness, but discusses a belief in a God found most clearly in nature, and in a religion that is a way of life.

Survival of the fittest, the balance of nature, and self-preservation are all linked in *Man of the Forest*. All of nature, including the human world, is involved in a struggle to survive, each trying to preserve its own life. Only those more powerful or cunning will be successful, and in this way, a balance can be maintained. As Grey's character, Milt Dale, proclaims: "Only the strongest an' swiftest survive. That is the meaning of nature. There is always a perfect balance kept by nature. It may vary in different years, but on the whole, in the long years, it averaged an even balance."[22] In this novel, the wild forest environment of the Tonto Basin, the Mogollon Rim, and the White Mountains—where trees and plants struggle to reach the sunlight and beasts kill each other to survive—symbolize the competition that permeates all life. Grey's emphasis of these themes reveals the extent to which the theories of Charles Darwin and Herbert Spencer impressed him.

The strongest philosophical message, and the theme of the entire novel, is that of reason versus instinct. Through this theme, reason is linked with the symbol of eastern thought and culture through Helen Raynor, while instinct is represented by the natural man of the West, Milt Dale. Dale's comments illustrate Grey's thoughts on the subject:

> Here I am, the natural physical man, livin' in the wilds. An' here you come, the complex, intellectual woman. Remember for my argument's sake, that you're here. An' suppose circumstances forced you to stay here. You'd fight the elements with me an' work with me to sustain life. There must be a great change in either you or me, accordin' to the other's influence. An' can't you see that the change must come in you, not because of anything superior in me—I'm really inferior to you—but because of our environment? You'd lose your complexity. An' in years to come you'd be a natural physical woman, because you'd live through an' by the physical.[23]

Instinct and reason battle again in several articles and short stories Grey produced on the theme of hunting in the Tonto Basin. Three serials published in *The Country Gentleman* detail Grey's bear hunting expeditions in the Tonto. The first, "Arizona Bear," began in the November 1920 issue of the magazine, and chronicles Grey's trip to the Tonto the previous year with Lee and Al Doyle; Babe, George, and Edd Haught; Grey's brother, R.C.; Sievert Nielson, Grey's friend; Ben Copple, a local prospector; and the Japanese cook, Takahashi. The second, "Bear Trails," appeared in two issues of *The Country Gentleman* in 1923, and describes Grey's 1922 adventures in the Tonto. The third series of articles, "Tonto Bear," sketches the events of Grey's 1923 excursion. For the most part, these articles were written to appeal to hunters and sportsmen and contain blow-by-blow descriptions of the hunt; one of them also attempts to analyze the attraction of hunting for the modern man.

In the sixth and final installment of "Arizona Bear," Grey examines the appeal of the hunt for those who abhor violence in their everyday lives. His analysis was prompted by an experience with a deer he had shot and fatally wounded. As he approached the stricken deer, the animal attempted to attack him, dragging its useless torso and hindlegs. Grey was struck by the expression in the deer's eyes of "only hate, only [the] terrible, wild, unquenchable spirit to live long enough to kill me!"[24]

He realized that the incident would require him to explore this "tendency of man to kill, . . . to try to analyze the psychology of hunting." After much thought Grey concluded that hunting represents a reversion to the savage, but that occasionally such a return is beneficial to both hunter and society.

> Hunting is a savage, primordial instinct inherited from our ancestors. It goes back through all the ages of man, and farther still—to the age when man was not man, but hairy ape, or some other beast from which we are descended. . . . We cannot escape our inheritance. Civilization is merely a veneer, a thin-skinned polish over the savage and crude nature. . . . Stealing through the forest or along the mountain slope, eyes roving, ears sensitive to all vibrations of the air, nose as keen as that of a hound, hands tight on a deadly rifle, we unconsciously go back. We go back to the primitive, to the savage state of man.[25]

When the hunter reverts, and stalks his prey, it is not an entirely negative situation. "After all," according to Grey,

> life is a battle. Eternally we are compelled to fight. If we do not fight, if we do not keep our bodies strong, supple, healthy, soon we succumb to some germ or other that gets a hold in our blood or lungs and fights for its life, its species, until it kills us. Fight, therefore is absolutely necessary to long life . . . manhood, strength—the symbols of fight! To be physically strong and well a man must work hard, with frequent intervals of change of exercise, and he must eat meat. I am not a great meat eater, but I doubt if I could do much physical labor or any brain work on a vegetable diet. Therefore I hold it fair and manly to go once a year to the wilderness to hunt. Let that hunt be clean, hard, toil, as hard as I can stand.[26]

Hunting requires the use of human instinct and the temporary surrender of reason, while it strengthens and invigorates the physical body. The chase, more than the kill, is the real value of hunting, as it places a person once more in a natural environment, pitting human wit against physical elements, beasts, and human frailty, and forces the hunter to meet the challenge of nature.

The thrill of the chase is celebrated in a short story entitled "The

Wolf Tracker," which has only two characters: a man named Brink, who is the wolf tracker, and the wolf, Old Gray. Old Gray had terrorized the range from Cibecue Creek to Mt. Wilson for years, always eluding capture; Brink becomes determined to end the wolf's days of slaughter. He tracks the animal through the winter, from October to April, but at every juncture, the wolf evades him. Brink stays on his trail, becoming increasingly impressed with the cunning of the wolf, and a strange relationship develops between the animal and the persistent tracker. Finally, the wolf is walked to death; exhausted, not allowed to rest, he no longer has the strength to survive. When offered reward money in return for Old Gray's pelt, Brink declines and disappears into the forest. The story is well written, superior to many of Grey's book-length works. It acknowledges the wild animal's instinctive will to survive, while celebrating the hunter's perseverance and the life and death struggle of the hunt.

A more humorous look at hunting is found in "Tonto Basin." This article was originally published in an anthology, *Tales of Lonely Trails* (1922), and describes Grey's 1918 expedition to the Tonto. Accompanying Grey for the first time is his oldest son, Romer, nine years old. Romer displays remarkable enthusiasm and energy for the hunt and is dismayed when deer elude him. He also finds delight in hunting wild turkey; his father and his Uncle R.C. collaborate with him on a wild turkey hunt. Romer's fresh point of view reminds Grey of his own youthful adventures and rekindles his interest in and enjoyment of hunting.

While hunting with the Haughts, Grey was entertained around the campfire with legends and stories of the Tonto. Always alert for material, he developed several of these tales into short stories, such as "Tappan's Burro" and "The Secret of Quaking-Asp Cabin."

"Tappan's Burro" explores the relationship between a prospector and his faithful burro, Jenet. Jenet saves Tappan's life once in Death Valley, and is, in all ways, the perfect companion for a prospector. When they are prospecting in the Superstition Mountains of southern Arizona, they encounter another party that includes a woman, and Tappan accompanies the group to their Tonto Basin ranch. He and the woman fall in love and plan to elope, but they have to leave Jenet behind. After only one day, the woman disappears with all Tappan's gold. Tappan trails the thieves for a year, finally returning to the Tonto where an older, thinner, battlescarred Jenet still awaits him. He vows never to leave her again. Many years later, Tappan saves Jenet's life by dragging her out of the high, snowy climes of the Tonto to a lower altitude where food is available, giving up his own life in the process. Like Grey's other short stories, this develops the themes of mutual dependence of man and animal in the West, loyalty, and self-sacrifice.

"The Secret of Quaking-Asp Cabin" uses as a setting a deserted log cabin in the Tonto. According to the story, Grey, while hunting, becomes separated from his companions. Searching for a way back to the camp in Beaver Canyon, he discovers a cabin, and, as it is getting late, decides to pass the night there. This proves to be a particularly harrowing experience; he falls prey to all kinds of imagined horrors (he even admits in print that he has always been afraid of the dark) and becomes convinced that some tragedy has occurred in the cabin. In the clear light of morning, he easily finds his way back to camp and his companions, and soon thereafter begins a search to uncover the cabin's secret.

According to Babe Haught, the cabin had been the site of a number of tragedies, and he tells Grey all he knows. The Hashknife outfit once used it as a campsite before turning to rustling. Tappan and his burro, Jenet, had lived there awhile, and it was there that Tappan lost his life. Grey is sure that these stories partly account for the atmosphere of the place, but thinks that there is more to be told. On his third hunting trip after his discovery of the cabin, he learns its secret.

The secret of Quaking-Asp Cabin is revealed to Grey by an Indian. According to this man, the cabin had been built by Richard Starke, his young bride, Blue, and his brother Len. The tale is one of adultery, guilt, jealousy, and vengeance. Blue fell in love with Len and they plotted Richard's murder. The plan failed, but Richard was severely injured. Len disappeared into the forest, while Blue, guilt ridden, tended a bitter Richard for five years. Hate and the desire to make her suffer were all that kept him alive, but the death of their child moved him to forgive his wife before he himself died.

The story has the flavor of Grey's nonfictional accounts as well as resemblances to his short stories. He includes authentic figures such as Babe Haught, his sons, and Takahashi, his cook. It is told in the first person and mentions locations with which Grey was familiar, such as the campsite at Beaver Canyon. Other elements of the story, such as accounts of rabid skunks and an episode in which a deer Grey had wounded tries to attack him, had previously appeared in other works and were apparently anecdotes that he liked to embellish and use over and over again. The inclusion of the Hashknife outfit, Tappan's burro, and the Indian who told the story of the cabin represent wholly fictional situations. This story lends even more credence to the supposition that Babe Haught was a rich source of Tonto Basin stories and legends, and is a fine example of the way Grey intermingled fact, fiction, and fancy in his writing.

An atypical story from the Tonto Basin is "The Kidnapping of Collie Younger." Published for the first time in 1976, this is the story of a young girl from Texas who has just graduated from the Flagstaff Normal School (now Northern Arizona University). Wild and flirtatious, she is surrounded by beaus, one of whom is so enamoured that he persuades his brother to kidnap and hold her captive in the Tonto Basin. This would allow him to rescue her, and become a hero in her eyes. The plot is duly carried out, and Collie Younger is abducted and taken to a lonely cabin in the Tonto. The plan is disrupted, though, when they encounter some bona fide gangsters who capture both of them. Collie's spunk and her pseudo-abductor's courage and ingenuity allow them to devise a means of escape. Then, further complicating the original plan, the two fall in love and the scheme backfires on the lovelorn brother who had concocted it in the first place.

This story falls into no clear category; evidently set in the 1920s or 1930s as suggested by the gangster element, it is a comedy of sorts but is also a love story. Nevertheless, it is set in the Tonto and indicates Grey's forays into experimentation with that area.

Grey loved the Tonto Basin and Mogollon Rim perhaps more than any area of Arizona, and the Tonto books reveal his deep regard for the area. It was there that he spent the most time, and a greater proportion of his western romances were set in that locale. Other environments pitted him against the challenge of a hostile and barren terrain and allowed him to address the question of man's adaptability to desolation, but the Tonto afforded him the opportunity to dramatize mankind's reactions to more pleasant surroundings.

The Tonto was the last of the four areas of Arizona Grey explored, both personally and in writing. All of his Arizona novels, regardless of where they were set, were popular among his readers, but by 1918, Grey was already intrigued with a new medium that could communicate his love of the land to a wider audience and in an even more dramatic fashion. He began to explore the possibilities of transferring his written words into visual images for the silver screen.

THE
SILVER SCREEN
AND BEYOND

CHAPTER IX

ZANE GREY AND THE
FILM INDUSTRY

While Zane Grey was completing his education, opening his dental practice, and learning to be an author, momentous changes were occurring in the area of popular entertainment. With the invention in 1895 of the Cinematographe by the Lumiere brothers and subsequent developments of Edison and Armat's Vitascope and William Dickson's Biographe, the production of motion pictures for the large screen had begun.[1] The Cinematographe, the Vitascope, and the Biographe all made their American debuts in 1896 in New York City, the same year that Grey established his dental practice there.[2]

The first motion pictures were brief and involved little in the way of plot or story line. Once the novelty of "moving pictures" dissipated, audiences soon tired of this limited entertainment, and filmmakers sought new ways to capture public interest in motion pictures. In France, George Melies produced over a thousand films, ranging from short subjects to longer productions with story lines; in the United States, Edwin W. Porter, impressed with Melies's work, also undertook the production of films that told stories.[3] His most famous work was *The Great Train Robbery,* made in 1903.

The Great Train Robbery was a milestone for both the film industry

and the western movie. It was not the first western, although it contained
many elements later associated with them and was the first such movie
with a recognizable form. It was, however, a huge commercial success
for its makers and indicated a profitable direction for the film industry.[4]
More importantly, *The Great Train Robbery* had a familiar theme. Train
robberies were still common in 1903, and the movie was a drama that attempted to recreate actual events as authentically as possible.[5]

Always aware of developments that might affect the popularity and
sale of his western novels, Grey became interested in this new industry.
By 1918, three of Grey's books had been made into movies. Also during
this year, he established a home at Altadena, California, close to industry offices, which had already migrated to the West Coast from New Jersey. Although Grey's motives for relocating had more to do with fishing
and being near Arizona, his presence in California made it convenient
for him—or more accurately, for his wife Dolly—to keep abreast of
cinematic developments and maintain a business relationship with movie
moguls.[6] Those early films represent the beginning of an association between Grey's work and the motion picture business that spanned five
decades and produced one hundred thirteen films.

Zane Grey's western romances were natural material for the budding
industry; features that appealed to readers were transferable to the visual
medium. Exotic settings in an enchanted land, noble heroes and chaste,
beautiful heroines, predictable plots in which good overcame evil, the
celebration of values perceived by the public to be distinctly American,
and above all, the overriding importance of the land, traveled easily
from the printed page to the silver screen. This movement enlarged the
already wide audience Grey reached through his novels, and communi-
cated his perception of the West to ever-increasing numbers of people.

The association between Grey and Hollywood began on an idyllic
note. Grey saw the film medium as a way in which his novels could
reach a vast audience in as authentic and original a form as possible, and
the motion picture industry cooperated with him in achieving that goal.
Beginning in 1918 and lasting until 1929, Grey's relationship with the
industry was a close one. His films were generally made on location,
featured the land that he felt was so important to the nature of the West,
and relied upon his suggestions.

Films related to the Arizona books played a major role in the total
volume of Grey's western romances dramatized for the screen. Of
the first three films, two were based on Arizona books and were made

in Arizona. This proportion continued: sixty-eight of the one hundred thirteen films—or almost two-thirds—were based on the Arizona novels, filmed in Arizona, or both. These films spanned the era of the silent movies and extended well into the age of sound. Between 1918 and 1929, thirty-two silent films related to Arizona were made. Almost all of these were black and white, though experimentation with color had begun as early as 1924.[7] Films produced during this first stage of the association between Zane Grey and Hollywood reveal Grey's close relationship with the producers. This was demonstrated by the care that film companies took to follow the books as closely as possible, by the fact that much of the filming took place at the locations where the stories were set, and by Grey's presence during the filming. These factors contributed to the fidelity of films made during this era and present Grey's vision, which rested upon the land at its center.

Fox Studios produced *Riders of the Purple Sage* and *The Rainbow Trail* in 1918; both featured William Farnum in the lead.[8] Plans for filming had been made beginning as early as February of 1916, but the actual work did not begin until May 1918. The company was in northern Arizona for three weeks shooting background footage for both films. Although Grey was not in Arizona during this period, the Fox company did remain in touch with him.[9]

After the Fox production of these first two films, Grey formed his own movie company. He had sold the motion picture rights for *Riders of the Purple Sage* and *The Rainbow Trail,* along with those for another book, *The Border Legion,* to William Fox for $2500 each in 1916.[10] While this represented a sizable amount of money for the era, Grey felt he could make even more if he produced the films himself and retained the profit from ticket sales. Accordingly, in 1919, he formed Zane Grey Productions in partnership with Benjamin H. Hampton.[11] Hampton was actually in charge of production, and Grey was only an occasional visitor to the offices. The company made seven motion pictures, four of which were based on Arizona titles.

Desert Gold was produced in 1919 by Zane Grey Productions, and most of the actual filming took place at Palm Springs, California.[12] Grey visited the location and was moved to comment upon the methods used in a letter to his partner, Hampton. He was most impressed with the way Hampton had recreated his book. "You have," he wrote, "put the spirit, the action, and the truth of 'Desert Gold' upon the screen."[13]

Grey's enthusiastic support of Hampton's methods was derived from his own perception of the proper relationship between the story, the medium, and the actors. The story itself was to be featured and faithfully duplicated without the distraction of a star who would twist it in order to accentuate his or her best abilities. "Your elimination of the star system is going to revolutionize the motion picture business," wrote Grey. "Just so long as stars insist on having all the strong scenes of a book, just so long will motion pictures be weak."[14] Grey was unwilling to share the limelight with anyone, even the actors who dramatized his characters. Always possessive, he was convinced that the medium should be of secondary importance to his stories, and that the actor's personality should be submerged in the characters he had created.

The star system was a relatively recent addition to the process of movie making; it seems to have originated in 1910, when Florence Lawrence, the "Biograph Girl," attracted crowds to films in which she appeared. People came for the sole purpose of watching her, regardless of the role she played. Mysterious events in her life, including newspaper reports of her supposed death, provoked public interest in her personality quite apart from her vocation as an actress. Grey disliked the star system and at one point was moved to express his perceptions of the system's weaknesses in a short story.

"On Location" was set on the northern Arizona Navajo Reservation and featured a movie crew engaged in filming a motion picture.[15] The two stars of the picture, Vera Van Dever and Bryce Pelham, were portrayed as vain manipulators and jealous cowards. The unknown stuntgirl and cowboy selected to stand in for Pelham surpass the stars in both courage and acting. In addition to Grey's obvious disapproval of the star system, clearly expressed in this story, the piece was interesting for its insight into the methods used in filming a story on location.

Zane Grey Productions filmed three more Arizona novels. *The U.P. Trail*—based on the book that featured Al Doyle's tales of the construction of the first transcontinental railroad—was produced in 1920, *Man of the Forest* in 1921, and *When Romance Rides* (retitled from *Wildfire*) in 1922. Grey considered moving his motion picture company to Arizona and headquartering it at Flagstaff to make these films, but this plan did not come to fruition. In all, Grey's excursion into filmmaking resulted in seven pictures and his discovery that he did not care to be closely involved with the film industry.[16] He bought Hampton's share of the company in 1922 and then sold the whole business to Jesse L. Lasky, one of the pioneers of the motion picture industry.[17]

In 1911, with partners Samuel Goldfish (later Goldwyn) and Cecil B. De Mille, Lasky acquired the rights to a successful Broadway play, *The Squaw Man*. The men hired one of New York's leading stage actors, William Farnum, to play the lead. At this time, most films were made outside where the light was better, but during the frigid eastern winters, filming was impossible. Consequently, when making *The Squaw Man*, Lasky and Farnum boarded the train for Arizona where they had been told that it was always filming weather. The train arrived in Flagstaff in the middle of a blizzard and without stepping foot off the train, Lasky decided to continue on to California. There *The Squaw Man* was made, the first motion picture produced entirely in Hollywood. Lasky's partnership, Famous Players–Lasky, later became known as Paramount Studios.[18]

After the production of *The Squaw Man*, Lasky's enthusiasm for western movies continued. When he bought Zane Grey Productions, he began a close association with Grey that resulted in the production of fifty-four movies based on Grey's novels, thirty-six of which were from the Arizona stories. Between 1922 and 1929, film contracts between Grey and Paramount Studios carried a clause that called for filming on the actual location as portrayed in the book.[19] This helped insure the fidelity of film to novel, and gave the land proper prominence. As early as 1923, Grey was personally escorting Lasky around the various scenic points of northern Arizona, such as Keams Canyon and Rainbow Bridge, in search of picturesque film backgrounds.[20] Additionally, Grey often visited the film locations and was consulted concerning appropriate ways to reproduce his stories.

The association between Grey and Paramount was a close and cooperative one, beneficial to both sides. Throughout the 1920s, Paramount paid $25,000 for the film rights to each novel they filmed; these were sold as seven-year leases and eventually reverted to the author, so Grey was able to retain control of them. Grey and Paramount split the profits from the films on an equal basis. Paramount productions of Grey's stories were of a higher quality than those developed by other companies, both because they provided a generous budget and because they built a unit that specialized in producing Zane Grey films.[21] This resulted in a series of movies of consistent quality. The use of Grey's name and his stories boosted ticket sales for Paramount, while the films enhanced the sale of his books.

Paramount filmed *To the Last Man* in 1923 with Richard Dix starring as Jean Isbel. The female lead was Lois Wilson, who played Ellen Jorth, and Noah Beery, Sr., noted for depicting villains, played Colter, one of the outlaws. After limited motion picture experience, Dix signed with Paramount as a contract player, and *To the Last Man* was one of his Paramount assignments. He was also among Grey's favorites. One evening Grey took his children to see a movie in which Dix starred, and subsequently wrote to Dolly (on a cruise to Europe) that

> we went to the movies last night, and took the kids. Luckily the show was decent. We saw Richard Dix (the man who's playing Jean Isbel in my Forest story) and I must say that I like him very much.[22]

Victor Fleming, who later became famous as the director of *Gone With the Wind,* directed the film.

To the Last Man was made during the summer of 1923 on location near Payson, Arizona, close to Pleasant Valley.[23] It was a remote location and posed quite a few problems in transporting cast, crew, equipment, and supplies to the site. All the necessary equipment—including cameras and their related gear—was packed in by horse, as were fifty to sixty of the people involved. Tent houses served as sleeping quarters for most of the crew, but Grey leased his lodge to the movie studio, and the more important persons used it as their headquarters. The Haughts, Grey's friends and hunting companions, handled many details for the movie people, including construction of corrals and barns to house the livestock, and tents for human shelter. They helped build a log cabin by Tonto Creek, and facilitated the construction of an entire town below Payson. Even more dramatic, a portion of a cliff wall was blasted away with their direction, blocking off a canyon to be used by the film's rustlers.

The Haughts also took an active part in the filming. Several of the children were used in some of the scenes, particularly one that involved a waterfall. One of the Haught's horses was even featured. This particular horse had mastered the trick of untying the rope on the corral gate and letting himself into the barn; several scenes of this feat were filmed.

Call of the Canyon was filmed by Paramount studios in and around Flagstaff in the fall of 1923.[24] Wilson and Dix again played the lead roles, Noah Beery, Sr., played the villain, and Ricard Cortez, a Latin lover from the same school as Rudolph Valentino, played a supporting role. Bebe Daniels was engaged to play the second female lead, but her feelings were hurt because she was not given the starring role. The script was wired to her in New York, but on her way back to the West Coast, she refused to get off the train when it stopped at Flagstaff. Contract player Estelle Taylor replaced her, but before the picture was finished, became ill and was replaced by Marjorie Daw. Victor Fleming directed.[25]

Some of the scenes for *Call of the Canyon* were filmed in Flagstaff. The train station was used for a scene in which Lois Wilson arrived in the West, and the Weatherford Hotel was featured as the place where the heroine stayed upon her arrival. Several local people participated as extras, notably the misses Lucretia McMullen and Katharine Beckwith, who donned riding costumes and rode their horses back and forth in front of the cameras.

Most of the movie was filmed in Oak Creek Canyon, the setting of the novel. The Thomas ranch was used for many of the scenes, although special provision had to be made for a scene that required a sand storm. Ultimately, the storm was filmed about fourteen miles east of Flagstaff, at Winona; three large airplane motors (two Stutz and one Liberty) with propellers were transported to the site. Technicians reversed the propellers, and started the engines, creating a believable sand storm for the camera. The only serious problem encountered during the filming in Oak Creek Canyon was a rainstorm, which delayed production for a few days. It did, however, provide an opportunity to introduce a flood scene.[26] Filmmaking in the early twenties was often a serendipitous activity.

Grey visited the filming of *Call of the Canyon* in September. Lasky met him in Flagstaff and the two toured northern Arizona in search of locations for future movies. Lasky was already planning to film *Heritage of the Desert* and *The Vanishing American* in Arizona. A bright and prosperous film future was predicted.[27]

Filming for *Heritage of the Desert* began at the end of September, before *Call of the Canyon* was completed. Lee Doyle was in charge of transporting supplies, equipment, and animals to Lee's Ferry, and received a long-term contract from Paramount Studios to provide services for their Arizona film crews. Bebe Daniels, who refused to play the second lead in *Call of the Canyon,* was signed for the lead female role of Mescal; Lloyd Hughes played Jack Hare, the male lead. A newcomer, James Mason, played Snap Naab, and a familiar face in Grey westerns, Noah Beery, Sr., played the villainous Holderness.[28]

Production of *Heritage of the Desert* was a large scale operation. Scenes for the movie were shot north of Flagstaff at The Gap, at the Cameron Bridge over the Little Colorado River, and at Lee's Ferry. Seventy Hollywood people were included in the film crew, along with fifty Indians and two thousand wild horses. Bebe Daniels was reported to be "roughing it" in a desert camp at Lee's Ferry with her mother and staff.

Upon his return from his desert tour with Jesse Lasky, Grey visited the filming. Publicity material for this movie quoted Grey saying: "Not until Paramount started producing my stories have I ever had any hand in supervising them for the screen. Regardless of what has been printed, that is the truth."[29] Grey urged the people of Flagstaff to build another hotel to accommodate the interests of the motion picture industry. His perception of the future relations between the industry and Arizona was evident in an interview with *The Coconino Sun:*

> An intense rivalry is already established between big motion picture producers to see which shall first get here and utilize the scores of attractions, scenic and ethnological, this section has to offer. They realize it is a virgin field. They are coming here in a drove to capitalize on it.[30]

As can be seen, Grey was very much involved in the filming of his novels in Arizona by Paramount Studios during this early period. As long as they were authentic reproductions of his stories, and were filmed at the actual locations, he was interested in their progress and success. Paramount Studios cooperated with him, accommodating his concerns and wishes.

Despite their idyllic relationship, Paramount did not have exclusive monopoly on Grey's pictures, and few of the films made by other companies accurately reproduced Grey's stories. The United Picture Theatres of America produced *The Light of Western Stars* in 1919 with Dustin Farnum in the lead role as Gene Stewart, but this movie was not made on location. Fox Studios had earlier purchased film rights to four of Grey's titles, including *The Lone Star Ranger* and *The Last of the Duanes,* as well as *Riders of the Purple Sage* and *The Rainbow Trail,* and these titles were filmed several times during the silent film era.[31]

The Lone Star Ranger, made by Fox in 1919, featured William Farnum as the lead. Although the novel was set in Texas, the remake was filmed by Fox in 1921 in Prescott, Arizona. It featured Fox's leading box office draw, Tom Mix, a stunt rider who had moved into the early motion picture business.[32] Fox Studios also remade *Riders of the Purple Sage* and *The Rainbow Trail* in 1925 with Tom Mix. He played the lead role in both films: Lassiter in *Riders of the Purple Sage* and Shefford in *The Rainbow Trail*. Neither film was in Arizona, and both were silent movies.

The plot of Fox's 1925 version of *Riders of the Purple Sage* was substantially different from the novel Grey wrote. In the film, Mix played a Texas Ranger who was seeking revenge against a lawyer named Lew Walters, who had abducted his sister. The film version had Mix becoming ramrod for Jane Withersteen's ranch, killing Walters, and escaping with Jane from a posse. Many of the intricacies of Grey's original story line were missing, including the Mormon element.

The plot of the 1925 version of *The Rainbow Trail* also differed from the novel. Tom Mix played the role of Shefford, while Lassiter and Jane were acted by Doc Roberts and Carol Holloway. While in this film, Shefford freed Lassiter and Jane from Paradise Valley, and rescued Fay Larkin from a forced marriage (not unlike the story found in Grey's novel), once again the omission of the Mormon element and the complete absence of any mention of polygamy in the film resulted in a movie version that was significantly different from the novel.

Although the Fox films diverged from the story line written by Grey, the film *Lightning,* produced by Tiffany Films in 1927, bore even less resemblance to anything Grey wrote. Evidently based upon Grey's short story of the same name, it featured the wild horse, Lightning, and the wild horse trackers of the Arizona Strip, Cuth and Lee Stewart. The Stewarts did appear in the film, but so did various female characters not in Grey's original story. Even more outrageous was a villain in the film named Simon Legree, a melodramatic character never used by Grey.

Paramount Studios continued with their own plans for the authentic reproduction of Grey's titles. Discussions on filming of *The Vanishing American* began as early as the fall of 1923 during the production of *Call of the Canyon*. It was to be done on a more lavish scale than any western to date, and would be a color production. A budget of $500,000 was mentioned, a figure soon inflated to $1 million. Filming was to take place at the Rainbow Bridge, Grand Canyon, and Kayenta, and director Victor Fleming, along with Paramount executives Lucien Hubbard and W. L. Griffith, spent two weeks touring the area with Lee Doyle during the summer of 1924 to select exact locations. Actual production was to begin in August of 1924, and it was estimated that it would require at least two months to complete. The plans were brought to a halt, and filming delayed, when Paramount studios refused to pay the price required for the use of one of the locations and the attendant transportation costs.[33]

In the meantime, Paramount continued with plans for other films. Grey's *Wild Horse Mesa* was shot at White Mesa, the Grand Canyon, Red Lake, and Kaibito in the spring of 1925. Horses were highlighted in this movie, often in dangerous ways. At the Grand Canyon, for example, Emory Kolb was asked to arrange for the rescue of a horse and rider after they dove off a cliff and into the Colorado River. Kolb advised against the stunt, and the feat was moved upriver where neither the waters of the Colorado River nor the cliff in question were as high. The sorrel who made the plunge over the cliff gained considerable attention, but the focus of the film was upon a creamy white horse named Greylock, owned and trained by Lee Doyle. This was the film that began a series of westerns featuring Rex, King of Wild Horses, played by Greylock and others. Unfortunately, during a stampede scene, several of the horses used in the film were injured.

The human cast of the film was also outstanding. Jack Holt, who after a stint in the military during World War I returned to Hollywood and signed with Famous Players–Lasky, played the male lead, and Billie Dove played the female lead. Noah Beery, Sr., was the villain, and Douglas Fairbanks, Jr., acted the part of the main character's brother. The director was George B. Sietz (who later created the Andy Hardy series).[34]

Paramount did a remake of *The Light of Western Stars* shot on location in southern Arizona's Superstition Mountains during the spring of 1925.[35] Jack Holt was again the main character, Gene Stewart, and Billie Dove played Majesty Hammond.

A third film made in Arizona in 1925 was *Code of the West*. Publicity material for this movie stated that Grey himself selected Payson, Arizona, as the scene for the filming, since the book was based on actual incidents that occurred there. The Haughts were closely associated with the filming of this movie, as they had been with *To the Last Man* in 1923. Again, several of the younger Haughts were in the film.[36]

Finally, during the summer of 1925, *The Vanishing American* was made. One hundred and fifty people migrated to northern Arizona to make the picture, and about one hundred local cowboys and thirty-five hundred Indians were used. George B. Sietz directed the film, and Richard Dix played the starring role as Nophaie. Lois Wilson was Marion Warner, Nophaie's Anglo lover, and Noah Beery, Sr., played Booker, the Indian agent. Filming took place at Kayenta, Rainbow Bridge, and Tuba City.[37] This film is regarded as one of the finest screen adaptations of Grey's novels made by Paramount.[38] With Grey's emphasis on the theories of Charles Darwin and Herbert Spencer, it was appropriate that the film opened with a quotation from Spencer's *First Principles,* which referred to the theory of survival of the fittest. The film remained faithful to Grey's plot and characterizations.

Drums of the Desert was filmed in Arizona in the spring of 1927.[39] Based upon the novel *Captives of the Desert* (originally *Desert Bound*), the story was changed somewhat. The novel indicted a crooked Indian trader who sold whiskey to the Navajos, whereas the film centered upon oil men who illegally took Indian land. Warner Baxter played the hero, John Curry; three hundred Navajos, two hundred Anglo extras, and one hundred horses were used in the project. Filming took place at The Gap and at Lee's Ferry.

Under the Tonto Rim, a novel based upon the experiences of the Haught family, was filmed by Paramount at Payson in the fall of 1927.[40] Grey was present during the filming, and once again, he and Lasky personally selected the shooting locations. This film featured a new leading man, Richard Arlen, one of Paramount's major attractions during the 1920s, who also starred in several subsequent remakes of earlier Grey films, including *The Border Legion* (1930), and *The Light of Western Stars* (1930). Arlen shared with Grey a love of fishing and was the author's personal friend.

By 1927, relations between Grey and the film industry were deteriorating. Grey stated in an interview with *The Coconino Sun* that he would "not say that all of the people in Hollywood are crooks, but I will say that all the crooks in Hollywood are in the motion picture industry."[41] He further characterized the men in the industry as "story pirates." The comment was made upon Grey's return from a hunting trip to Payson, where *Under the Tonto Rim* was being filmed, in reaction to Paramount's growing tendency to film his stories in Hollywood rather than at the stories' actual locations, and toward changing characters and story line. Despite this tension, Paramount continued to film his novels, and, at least throughout 1928, returned to Arizona for the filming.

The Water Hole, a film based on the novel *Lost Pueblo,* was filmed in Arizona in the summer of 1928.[42] The indoor scenes were done in Hollywood, with only the outdoor portions shot on location. Kayenta, Monument Valley, and Betatakin House Ruins were the sites for this film, which, like the novel on which it was based, focused on the love story of a young archeologist and a spoiled eastern socialite. Jack Holt played archeologist Phillip Randolph, while Nancy Carroll acted the role of Judith Endicott, the female lead.

Excitement surrounded the production of *Avalanche,* based upon Grey's short story of the same name. Made during the late summer and early fall of 1928, the cast included Jack Holt and the Russian actress, Olga Baclanova. Actors and crew made their headquarters at the Monte Vista Hotel, while the actual filming was done at various places in the vicinity of Flagstaff. Several scenes, utilizing one hundred and fifty Indians, were made at Lake Mary. The most difficult scenes to film were those shot in the crater of the San Francisco Peaks, an altitude of twelve thousand feet. To reach that almost inaccessible site, a trail three quarters of a mile in length was constructed, over which cameras, equipment, and people were transported on horseback.[43]

The last of the silent Paramount pictures filmed on location was *Sunset Pass,* made in the late fall of 1928. Headquarters for the film crew was Tuba City, and filming took place there and in Blue Canyon, to the north, where a stampede of cattle was photographed.[44] During overcast days, when filming outside was impossible, the movie crew turned the dining room of a guest ranch in Tuba City into a cowboy bunkhouse, and shot several scenes there. The front of a home in Moencopi, used by missionaries to the Hopis, became the cinematic home of the Preston family, the center of the film's story.

The plot was fairly consistent with the story written by Grey. In the novel, Trueman Rock was a cowboy who returned to the town of Wagontongue where he fell in love with Thiry Preston and followed her to her ranch. He discovered that her father and brother were cattle thieves, and he endeavored to end their outlawry while winning Thiry's love. The plot of the film was similar to that of the novel, except that the character's names were changed slightly (Jack Rock and Leatrice Preston), and Rock was made a marshal who went to the Preston ranch to uncover a suspected rustling ring.

Seventy-five people were in the cast and crew of *Sunset Pass,* and several weeks were spent in Tuba City making the film. Jack Holt, who had been in Arizona just a few months before filming *Avalanche,* played

Jack Rock. Nora Lane played Leatrice Preston, and Englishman John Loder played her brother, Ash. An unexpected snowfall halted filming for a few days, but the cast entertained themselves with a snowball fight, which was captured on film.

A remake of *The Light of Western Stars* was the last of the silent films of Grey's Arizona novels. The story had been filmed twice before, once in 1919 by United Picture Theatres of America, and once in 1925 by Paramount Studios. This version was made by Paramount and cast Richard Arlen in the main role. Other characters in this film, Pie Pan Pultz, Bob Drexell, Stack, and Square Toe, had not appeared in Grey's novel of the same name. The film diverged from Grey's book as well in that it was not filmed at the location where the story took place, but was made in a Hollywood studio. This divergence foretold the nature of the relationship between his original works and the films that were made from them during the era of sound production.

With the last of the silent films of Grey's Arizona novels, an era ended in the history of the cinema. During the silent film era, much of what the industry produced was spontaneous and experimental in nature. This was reflected in Grey's Arizona films, where cast and crew often took advantage of unforeseen events, such as rain, to add scenes to the movies that were not in the original novel but added a touch of freshness to the story. Making movies was frequently a strenuous, demanding, and sometimes dangerous occupation, but filming was an adventure, and as the industry and the medium were new, had the characteristics of a pioneering, groundbreaking enterprise.

With the last of the silent films, a stage had ended in the relationship between Grey and the film business as well. During the silent-film era, the medium was considered to be secondary in importance to the story, and thus efforts were made to produce movies faithful to the plots and characters created by Grey. Grey himself encouraged this approach by insisting that the movies made of his books be filmed on location, and reproduce almost exactly what he had written. Because his perception of the West so intimately integrated the land, this concern strengthened the movies' ability to reproduce Grey's concepts. Also during this era, Grey was closely involved in the filming of his novels, and frequently visited locations and helped in the site selections for the actual filming. Because of the close cooperation between Grey and the motion picture studios, these movies very closely resembled the western romances he wrote, and dramatized the image of Arizona and the West that Grey perceived and recreated in his novels. This amicable relationship did not continue into the era of sound production.

Films made after 1930 remained popular with audiences, as evidenced by Hollywood's continued production of them, but Grey's direct involvement in their production decreased dramatically, and the movies themselves contained less and less resemblance to the romances he had written. The total output of "talking" Arizona films numbered thirty-six, slightly more than the thirty-two silents, but the later films did not have Grey's personal touch. With some few exceptions, they were no longer shot on location, thus altering the prominent role that the land played in Grey's fiction. Film content, in terms of plot and character, also changed dramatically from Grey's original work.

Nonetheless, the spirit of Grey's West remained. Heroes still wore white, and were loyal, honest, and true. Villains wore black and were thoroughly despicable. Women were pretty and virtuous, and the setting, even if not exactly duplicating Grey's, still featured the landscape of the West and attempted to communicate the land's magnificence. Above all, the name of Zane Grey was on the marquee. Although at times this seemed to be the only connection the films had with the novels, Grey's name alone drew audiences, who came expecting a good story, one with a plot that reaffirmed their ideals and values and emphasized the western environment. This expectation was derived from Grey's stories, and is the legend of Zane Grey.

Relations between Grey and the film studios deteriorated throughout the 1930s. There had previously been some tension between him and the studios, aggravated no doubt by his avowal in 1927 that all crooks in Hollywood were in the film industry, and by his labeling of film people as "story pirates."[45] There were other reasons as well for the strained relations. Grey insisted that the films remain true to the plot and to the characters he created and that they be filmed on the locations where he had set the story. Changes in his work irritated him. Both Paramount and Fox studios accommodated Grey during the silent film era, and the resulting fidelity of movie to book was used as publicity, as was Grey's association with the production of the film. Beginning in the 1930s, however, the studios faced the challenge of making a profitable new movie out of stories that had already appeared on the screen once, and in some cases, more than once. To draw the audience, they varied the action and attractions, and sometimes the settings.

Grey's break with Arizona also affected his relations with the film industry. In 1930, after a disagreement with the Arizona Game Commission officials the previous year, Grey vowed never again to visit the state. Although six movies were made in Arizona after that date, Grey's self-imposed exile made it impossible for him to participate in production, and it was awkward for him to continue to insist that films of his books be made in Arizona. With his absence from the set of these films, and with his resulting inability to participate in the filming of his stories, Hollywood was free to make changes it deemed necessary to attract audiences.

The Depression of the 1930s affected films as well. There was a slump in the movie market in the early years of the decade that made changes in production practices necessary. To minimize production costs, films were shot on soundstages, or, if location work was mandatory, on sites more accessible than Arizona. The use of Hollywood personalities, or stars, was also used to draw audiences, and many later films of Grey's work were primarily vehicles for particular actors. Under this policy, the story was usually regarded as less important than the actor.[46]

This is clearly demonstrated in the Fox series of westerns, in which a young actor named George O'Brien was featured. Eleven of these were based on novels by Grey, and six were screen adaptations of Arizona books. All sound productions, they represented Fox's move into the talking era.[47]

Associated with the film industry during the silent era as an assistant cameraman with the Tom Mix film production unit, and later as a stuntman, O'Brien was Fox studio's leading western actor in the thirties. The son of the San Francisco chief of police, O'Brien drifted into acting but soon became a foremost western star.[48]

O'Brien's first Zane Grey Arizona film was *The Lone Star Ranger*, made for Fox in 1929, but not released until 1930.[49] The film was based upon the novel of the same name, which Fox had already made twice (in 1919 and in 1921), but this was the first time it was made with sound. Much of it was filmed on location in Arizona at Rainbow Bridge, Monument Valley, Winslow, Tuba City, and Kayenta.

Grey visited the film company during the production. (Although he did not know it at the time, it was his last trip to Arizona.) After an extended tour of Utah and northern Arizona, and before going to his lodge in Payson for some hunting, Grey and the film's director, R. E. Houck, traveled together to Rainbow Bridge to select specific film sites, and the author spent several days with the film's cast and crew.[50]

Shortly afterward, in 1930 and 1931, Fox studios filmed three additional titles in Arizona with George O'Brien: *The Last of the Duanes, Riders of the Purple Sage,* and *The Rainbow Trail. Riders of the Purple Sage* was a big-budget production for which a complete replica of a Mormon village was constructed near Sedona. The entire village was set aflame at the end of filming, and its fiery destruction was recorded on film, complete with sound, for use in the movie. *Rainbow Trail* was filmed in and around the Grand Canyon in the fall of 1931.[51]

The success of these three films relied heavily upon the drawing power of O'Brien as the star, but they also counted upon Grey's name to attract audiences, and continued to strive for an authentic reproduction of Grey's work. Grey was directly involved in the production of *Lone Star Ranger,* even visiting the location site. Both *Riders of the Purple Sage* and *The Rainbow Trail* followed the general story line of the novels on which they were based, and if the filming did not occur at the exact spot where Grey set the novel, at least it was in the general vicinity. Nevertheless, it was clear that Hollywood used the films to promote the career of their western star while relying upon the film's association with Grey to sell tickets.

Three later films featuring George O'Brien and Zane Grey's story lines illustrate the tendency to move away from accurate reproduction and emphasize personality. In 1932 and 1934, Fox made three Grey movies: *Robber's Roost, Smoke Lightning,* and *The Dude Ranger.*[52] *Robber's Roost,* based on a novel set in the Green River area of central Utah, was filmed near Flagstaff in the fall of 1932. *Smoke Lightning* was from a short story entitled "Canyon Walls," and was set in a small Mormon village in southern Utah, but filmed in northern Arizona later that same year. *The Dude Ranger* had appeared in serial form in *McCall's Magazine* in 1931 (but not published as a novel until 1951). This time, although it was filmed in Zion National Park, the story was set in Arizona. The use of scenic backgrounds remained important to the films, but the filmmakers were no longer concerned with exact locations.

In response to Fox's success with George O'Brien, Paramount released a series of westerns with their own star, Randolph Scott. In this series, over twenty films were made based on Grey's books, and six were of the Arizona romances. Like Fox's productions, these were all "talkies." *Heritage of the Desert,* filmed in 1931, was the first, followed by *Wild Horse Mesa* (1932), *Sunset Pass* (1933), *Man of the Forest* (1933), *To the Last Man* (1933), and *Home On the Range* (1935). All were remakes of silent films of the 1920s, and all, except the last, were directed by Henry Hathaway.

Whether it was the director, the star, or a combination of the two that was responsible, Paramount's westerns managed to capture the spirit of Grey's novels. Scott himself, more than any other actor of the time, was identified as the true Grey hero. Like so many of Grey's main characters, Scott was an easterner who came west for his health. The climate agreed with him, and he began his acting career in amateur California theatrics. He later signed as a contract player for Paramount and began the western series.[53] The six Arizona films were not made on location; because they were remakes of silent films and Paramount needed to minimize production costs, Hathaway used location footage from the earlier films. Hathaway also took pains to create film heroes and heroines who reflected the novels' characters, although he did sometimes change names and characters.[54] Because of their reliance on footage from earlier films, the Arizona scenery, an actor who fell naturally into the pattern of the Grey hero, and a director who was concerned with recreating the spirit of the novels, these Paramount westerns were eminently successful.

The next Paramount series released could not boast these same advantages. Following the Randolph Scott films, Paramount produced westerns that starred Larry "Buster" Crabbe.[55] Three were based on Grey's Arizona novels: *Nevada* (1935), *Drift Fence* (1936), and *Desert Gold* (1936). Two more were based on novels set in other parts of the West, but the film version linked them with Arizona. Those were *The Arizona Raiders* (1936) based on *Raiders of the Spanish Peaks,* a novel set in Colorado, and *Arizona Mahoney* (1936) based on one of Grey's Death Valley tales, *Stairs of Sand.* None of Crabbe's movies were filmed in Arizona, and, with the exception of *Nevada,* a portion of which was filmed at Big Bear, California, none had any location work at all. The films had few characters that were directly from the novels and the story lines differed substantially from those in the original versions. Grey's name was used in the publicity material for the films, but it was clear that the producers were relying upon their star and the commercial qualities of Grey's name to draw audiences, and were not interested in creating authentic reproductions of his work. In spite of the discrepancies between the Crabbe films and Grey's novels, the public still received a movie that reflected the type of western they associated with Zane Grey.

Many western films made during the 1930s were of the "B" category, which indicated a lower budget for production and shorter length. After the slump of the early thirties, which increasingly moved the industry toward inexpensively made "B" westerns, the musical western became popular. This trend was reflected by a travesty of Grey's work entitled *Roll Along, Cowboy* (1937), a musical remake of *The Dude Ranger*. The fad was short-lived, and by the late thirties the conventional western enjoyed renewed popularity.

By the late thirties also, both Fox and Paramount studios discontinued the practice of producing long series of Grey westerns centered upon one screen personality. Instead, the films, which were a staple of the industry, introduced such actors as John Wayne (*Born to the West*, 1937), and Robert Mitchum (*Nevada*, 1937), who quickly rose to stardom and appeared in the studio's more lavish productions. Fox Studios (which became Twentieth Century Fox in 1935 when they merged with Twentieth Century Company), used their fourth and final remakes of both *Riders of the Purple Sage* (1941) and *The Last of the Duanes* (1941) to launch the career of their newest western discovery, George Montgomery, and RKO Radio publicized their featured western actor, James Warren, in two films, *Sunset Pass* (1946) and *Code of the West* (1947), both remakes. RKO also filmed three of Grey's titles with Tim Holt, son of actor Jack Holt who had appeared in many of Grey's silent westerns. Holt's films were not used to introduce him, as he was already RKO's most famous cowboy.[56] The three films, *Thunder Mountain (To the Last Man)*, *Under the Tonto Rim*, and *Wild Horse Mesa*, were all Arizona tales made in 1947. Although none of the storylines followed the novels exactly, the last two were shot on location in Utah, and all three presented stories and characters that were not dissimilar to those Grey had created. In all of these films, the studios endeavored to give the public the type of entertainment they expected from a Zane Grey story: valiant men, plenty of action, and beautiful scenery.

The late thirties and early forties also saw a series of Grey films in which the director was the main attraction.[57] Harry "Pop" Sherman, who arrived in Hollywood in the late twenties after a career as a film distributor, was hired to do the all-talking remake of *The Light of Western Stars* for Paramount in 1930. Instead he moved almost immediately into the project that brought him his greatest fame, the production of a series of films based on Clarence E. Mulford's Bar 20 Hopalong Cassidy books. In the late thirties, Paramount asked him to take over their Zane Grey series, and Sherman produced four films, three of which were Arizona titles: *The Mysterious Rider* (1938), *Heritage of the Desert* (1939), and *The Light of Western Stars* (1940). *The Mysterious Rider* was filmed during the spring of 1938 in Saguaro National Monument outside of Tucson, Arizona. Sherman did not use any of the previous films made from these novels for reference. As a consequence, these Grey films stand above those of the rest of the era. In them, he used what was known as his western formula, which stressed the opening and the ending, and let the middle fend for itself. Nevertheless, Sherman's films of Grey's works were the best that were produced in the late thirties and early forties. After more than twenty years of adapting Grey's books to the screen, the standard of quality was still the accuracy with which the film reproduced Grey's original story.

Even so, by the end of the decade, neither the Paramount nor Fox studios paid much attention to original settings, characters, or story lines of the novels, although they continued to create western films that had the flavor of Grey's stories. The growing discrepancy between the films and the novels was caused not only by the economic pressures of the Depression, but also by repeated use of the same titles, which made innovation in characters and plots necessary to attract audiences.

As Grey's health declined, his wife, Dolly, continued negotiations with the movie studios regarding film rights to his novels. Without Grey's active presence, even behind the scenes, the trend for the films to deviate from the novels increased.

The decade of the forties ushered in far-reaching changes. Sherman's four entries concluded Paramount's releases in 1940. Fox's fourth and final remakes of *Riders of the Purple Sage* and *The Last of the Duanes* in 1941 were the last of their Grey movies. RKO Radio produced a series beginning in 1944 with Robert Mitchum's *Nevada* and continuing with films starring James Warren made in 1946 and 1947. The 1947 Tim Holt series concluded RKO's venture into Zane Grey westerns. A suit filed by Grey's heirs agains RKO concerning contractual obligations was the primary reason given for their decision to stop filming the Grey titles entirely, but the fact that all the titles the studios owned had been remade numerous times was probably more decisive.[58] While the public continued to enjoy westerns that had the flavor and values found in Grey's stories, it was increasingly difficult to satisfy standards of authenticity while attracting with variety.

The few films based on Grey's romances released in the late forties and early fifties demonstrated the industry's new approach to draw audiences into the theatres. Only four Zane Grey films were produced in this time period, three of which—*Red Canyon* based on *Wildfire* (1949), *Robber's Roost* (1955), and *The Vanishing American* (1955)—were Arizona-related titles. The fourth and final film was *The Maverick Queen,* made by Republic in 1956. None of these bore a direct relationship to the novels whose titles they displayed. Although they retained the characters, or at least their names, found in the novels, the storylines were altered to cater to the tastes of the 1940s' and 1950s' audiences, who preferred films with rather simple, streamlined plots.

The emergence of two different types of westerns in the post–World War II era was another factor that heavily influenced the Zane Grey western films. A new breed of directors, such as Sam Peckinpah, produced movies that used the setting, costume, and time period of the conventional western to critique modern America. Films such as *High Noon* (United Artists, 1952) dramatized disillusionment with the nation and its values. Grey's books, as they were written, did not lend themselves to this approach, as his stories reaffirmed America's values and ideals.

Side by side with the films of social commentary, more conventional westerns continued to be made, in which good and evil were clearly distinct from each other, action and scenery dominated, and the films optimistically dramatized a world where the good guys always won. These, of course, were well within the Zane Grey tradition, which lived on in westerns made in the fifties and sixties, though the studios had exhausted Grey's original stories and began to use those of other authors or hired screenwriters to manufacture the type of plot required.

During the fifties, the Zane Grey tradition moved into a growing visual medium, television. Beginning in 1956, and continuing for five years, television viewers could tune in to one-hour action adventure tales on the Zane Grey Theatre, hosted by Dick Powell. This program was the result of an arrangement between Zane Grey Incorporated and Four Star productions. The one hundred twenty-nine episodes were not all based on Grey's original works, but they did feature western outdoor action and adventure stories of the same nature as those found in Grey's writing. The series was popular: Grey's name was used unabashedly to attract viewers who still thrilled to his brand of story-telling. The show remained in the twenty most frequently watched programs as indicated by the Nielsen polls, during its entire five-year run.

Zane Grey did not live to see his work translated into hour-long vignettes, available to every family with a television set in its living room. Moreover, his reaction to some of the adaptations undergone by his stories would probably have been bombastic. The durability of Grey's literary creations, however, is solid evidence of their intrinsic appeal to mainstream America, and the basis of the Zane Grey legend.

CHAPTER X

THE LEGEND OF
ZANE GREY

Zane Grey became a legend within his own lifetime. While he created his particular vision of the American West, he became a part of the picture, and his name came to represent the overpowering majesty of the western lands. It evoked heroes who embodied western traits, which he himself defined as endurance, manliness, loyalty, and courage. It summoned visions of heroines who were beautiful and chaste, and pictures of the land that was both backdrop and theme of his work. This legend grew after his death in 1939 and has endured for over forty years. His literary celebration of the West is evident in the evolution of films made from his stories, the continued prominence of his name in the field of western writing, and his widespread fame.

Grey's activities were severely limited after he suffered a stroke in 1937 while on a fishing expedition in Oregon; he only slowly recovered the use of his voice and limbs.[1] Always an extraordinarily active man, he was sixty-five years of age at the time. Just a year earlier, he had written to his friend, Alvah James:

> My future plans call for more research, more labor, more concentration on each novel than ever before. It is the way I have

lived and felt and worked and fished that has kept me young. I am a better fisherman than I ever was. This last week I beat Loren and Romer, and Loren's pal Gus, most decisively at tennis, and they are supposed to be good. Tennis, as you know, takes speed, eyesight, endurance, and intelligence. I have no bad habits, I don't eat much, and am chary of meats.

Please forgive this long dissertation about myself. I find an excuse in that your letter incited it.

Of course all this cannot last forever. But so far I have found no let-down and I'll achieve much before it wanes.[2]

Though he did not wish to limit his activities, his health demanded that he do so. For the last two years of his life, he did the things he enjoyed most, such as fishing. While he continued to write, he confined his relationship with the film industry to the business aspects of selling or leasing the motion picture rights to his novels. Dolly, as usual, handled the details.

After his death in 1939 of a heart attack, Grey's heirs assumed control of his work.[3] Dolly was primarily responsible for the continued publication of his books and the release of unpublished manuscripts, of which there were quite a few: thirty-five western romances were published before his death, but twenty-one were released afterward. Following Dolly's death in the 1950s, the eldest son, Romer Zane, assumed control of the corporation. When he died, control passed to the younger son, Loren, who monitors it today.

Evidence of Grey's widespread and longlasting fame is rampant. One indication is the stream of visitors to his cabin near Payson, Arizona. Built in 1920, the cabin was vacant from 1930 until 1963, when a Phoenix businessman, William H. Goettl, bought and renovated it, restoring the cabin's interior and exterior to the way it was when Grey stayed there. Today, it is managed by Margaret Sell and welcomes visitors between April and October each year. Grey's fans from as far away as Australia, Germany, Yugoslavia, France, Ireland, Czechoslovakia, Malaysia, New Zealand, and Peru have visited the cabin, although the majority of the visitors are from the United States, people who have read Grey's books and are interested in the man who wrote them.[4]

The continued fame of Grey is nowhere more evident, however, than in the enduring popularity of his western romances. Billed as "the American West's greatest storyteller," over one hundred thirty million copies of his books have been sold, and continue to sell. In bookstores, libraries, drugstores, grocery stores, in fact, any place where there are books, the prospective reader will find Grey titles on the shelves. Since their first publication by Harper and Brothers, the books were reprinted by Grossett and Dunlap in the thirties, and since the fifties, by Walter J. Black. Beginning in 1960, the western romances were reissued in paperback by Simon and Schuster (Pocket Books) and by Bantam Books. They have also been released by publishers Hamisch Hamilton and White Lion in England, and by Pendragon House in Canada. One of the most popular of the novels, *Nevada,* has been printed thirty-five times by six different publishing houses.[5] Translated into twenty-four languages, these romances have had high foreign sales, particularly in England, Germany, and the Scandinavian countries. In addition, Grey's books sell in Czechoslovakia, South Africa, South America, Holland, Italy, Israel, and Spain, and have even been translated into Annamese for distribution in Indochina. They are, however, banned in the Soviet Union. This lengthy and widespread printing history is a publishing response to the lucrative market for Grey's books.[6]

Much of Grey's appeal lies in his practice of basing stories on his own experiences. When he described a particular canyon, desert, forest, or mountain, his descriptions were believable because he was writing of what he had observed. His characterizations of cowboys, homesteaders, prospectors, and even outlaws bore the stamp of authenticity: in them, he was recreating people he had met on his trips to Arizona. When he told of a tenderfoot's aches and pains after a day in the saddle, or of thoughts and feelings upon first sighting natural wonders such as the Grand Canyon, Rainbow Bridge, Monument Valley, or the Painted Desert, the accounts were vivid and credible because he was recording his own thoughts and sensations. Although he often exaggerated both beauty and evil for dramatic effect, and endowed his characters with qualities reminiscent of the folklore that already surrounded them, he nevertheless infused first-hand knowledge into his portrait of the West. This penchant for detail and accuracy in geography, characterization, and sensation gave his stories interest and vitality, and enabled the reader to visualize and vicariously experience the adventures and the land of which he wrote.

Zane Grey's Arizona was not a kind land, but a harsh environment that demanded adaptability or death. The highest laws were competition, survival of the fittest, and the balance of nature. Within this context, humans and animals struggled for life, and in the struggle, developed traits and characteristics that symbolized their own adaptation to their surroundings. Each adaptation was unique. The Mormons on the high desert of the Arizona Strip reacted to the harshness of their existence by creating a predatory social system, one that was as fierce as the land that surrounded them. Their isolation allowed the strong to exploit the weak, and a society developed in which individual welfare was subordinated to that of the group. Only with the encroachment of civilization did the most severe elements of the society fade.[7] The Indians developed a religion and a way of life that was closely attuned to the land. Only when Anglo civilization intruded did their ways become anachronistic. The Mexicans in the southern borderlands were overwhelmed by their surroundings in Grey's stereotypical version, and in the face of the land's harshness, retreated into indolence, alcohol, and apathy. Cowboys, homesteaders, Indian traders, government agents, missionaries, hunters, rustlers, prospectors, outlaws, and gunmen: each evolved their own accommodation to the environment's demands.

Regardless of the effect, every individual who encountered the wilderness was subject to its influence. This became the hallmark of Grey's work. He once wrote:

> Places were the most vital and compelling things in the world, next to human life. Perhaps they were more important, because they had evolved life and had sustained it through the course of the ages. Whatever happened to people—birth, growth, trouble, defeat or success, love, passion, joy, loss, death—all were vitally affected by the part of the earth in which they took place.[8]

The adaptive process enforced individualism, another key element in Grey's portrait of the West. The result was a group of people who embodied the traits of that land: strength, independence, endurance, courage.

Grey himself was profoundly affected by the West. When he arrived in Arizona in 1907, he was an unknown author. Recognizing the potential of the Arizona setting, he utilized its attractions in his books. His instinct proved correct, and he became successful, admired by his readers. Wealth generated by his book sales enabled him to adopt a life of ease and leisure, and his existence became increasingly complex: sycophants surrounded him and he accumulated numerous material possessions. To regain his inspiration and zeal, he returned to Arizona where the primitive life, hard work, and the land itself restored him. He continued to believe his own idealization, even though he himself became a sophisticated man of the world.

Ironically, Grey's decision to leave Arizona was caused by this very relationship. From his first discovery of Arizona, he was charmed by its natural beauty, ruggedness, desolation, and isolation. He loved it all the more because the world had not yet discovered it and it could be his own paradise. Grey felt that he had learned about the West from true frontiersmen such as Buffalo Jones, Jim Emett, and Al Doyle, men who had opened doors for him to the different faces of Arizona. Grey had explored these areas and channeled all they had to offer into his novels, which introduced millions of people to the splendor of Arizona and the West. Many of these people then wanted to see for themselves the land about which he wrote so vividly, and visitors to Arizona increased. With them, they brought the trappings of civilization as well as its problems, all things Grey was trying to avoid.

As the land filled with the curious who had no true regard for it, the people and the atmosphere of Arizona altered. The oldtimers, from whom Grey had originally heard the stories of the Old West, were gone, replaced by people who knew little of the old days and were more concerned with the future than the past. Cowboys were indistinguishable from ordinary workmen. Schools, churches, and modern hotels took the place of saloons and the jailhouse. Automobiles, rather than stagecoaches or horses, carried the traveler down Arizona roads. Although he knew change was inevitable and that, in a sense, he himself had accelerated the process, Grey bemoaned the frontier's passing.

Grey's twenty-three-year relationship with Arizona proved profitable for both him and the state. Using plots, themes, and characters he found in Arizona, he created an image that fascinated readers. Through his books and stories, they could escape from their complicated modern lives and retreat to a simpler existence. This fictional Arizona, however, was seen through Grey's eyes and colored by his values. While his portrait of Arizona and the West was based on his experiences in that region, it would be a mistake to conclude that what he drew was an accurate depiction. He saw the shadow of the Old West, not its substance, a shadow cast by the remnants of frontier days that were vanishing even as he discovered them. Enchanted with this fading glimpse, he used it to construct his version of the nature of Arizona and the West, which was essentially his vision of what the world ought to be, based upon his idea of what the West had been.

An idealized West was the legend Zane Grey created in his books, the legend for which his own name has become symbolic. It is said of him:

> He may be no Henry James, Bret Harte, or Stephen Crane, but in the short run, at least, his impact on the American folk mind has been greater than that of those three, or of any other contemporary trio of authors combined. When you think of the West, you think of Zane Grey.[9]

Grey's vision of the West presented a golden era in America's past. Besieged by the complexities of twentieth-century life, his readers still look fondly toward his West for reaffirmation of their ideals.

NOTES

Unless otherwise specified, all references to "Grey" refer to Zane Grey

INTRODUCTION

1. These figures were arrived at from a list provided by Zane Grey Incorporated, entitled *Books by Zane Grey* (November 1979); Kenneth W. Scott, *Zane Grey: Born to the West* (Boston: G. K. Hall, 1979), 5–28.

2. Henry Nash Smith, *Virgin Land: The American West as Symbol and Myth* (Cambridge, Mass.: Harvard University Press, 1950), 3–4.

3. Grey's early life is documented in his autobiographical account, "My Own Life," in *Zane Grey: The Man and His Work* (New York: Harper and Brothers, 1928); Frank Gruber, *Zane Grey* (New York: Signet Books, 1970); Carlton Jackson, *Zane Grey* (Boston: Twayne Publishers, 1973); Jean Kerr, *Zane Grey, Man of the West* (New York: Grosset and Dunlap, 1949); Ann Ronald, *Zane Grey* (Boise, Idaho: Boise State University Press, 1975); Norris Schneider, *Zane Grey: The Man Whose Books Made the West Famous* (Zanesville, Ohio: Norris Schneider, 1967). Grey's birthplace was named for his maternal great-grandfather, Colonel Ebenezer Zane, a hero of the American Revolution and the settlement's founder.

4. Richard Hofstadter, *Social Darwinism in American Thought* (Boston: Beacon Press, 1944), 4, 13–24.

5. Ibid., 43–50.

6. Frederick Jackson Turner, "The Significance of the Frontier in American History," in *The Turner Theses: Concerning the Role of the Frontier in American History,* ed. George Rogers Taylor (Lexington, Mass.: D. C. Heath, 1972), 3–28.

7. Richard Etulain, "Cultural Origins of the Western," in *Focus on the Western,* ed.

Jack Nachbar (Englewood Cliffs, N.J.: Prentice-Hall, 1974), 19–24.

8. William E. Leuchtenburg, *The Perils of Prosperity: 1914–1932* (Chicago: University of Chicago Press, 1958), 1–11; Etulain, "Cultural Origins," 21–23.

9. Roderick Nash, *The Nervous Generation: American Thought, 1917–1930* (Chicago: Rand McNally, 1970), 1–4.

10. Alice Payne Hackett, *Eighty Years of Best Sellers: 1895–1975* (New York: R. R. Bowker, 1977).

11. These points are clearly evident in Grey's fiction, especially *The Vanishing American* (1925) and *Call of the Canyon* (1924).

CHAPTER 1: THE CANYON

1. Gruber, *Zane Grey,* 49–56.

2. For a thorough, scholarly consideration of Lee's Ferry and the people who lived near it, see Nels Anderson, *Desert Saints: The Mormon Frontier in Utah* (Chicago: University of Chicago Press, 1966); Charles S. Peterson, *Utah* (New York: W. W. Norton, 1977).

3. Grey, "The Man Who Influenced Me Most," *American Magazine,* August 1926, 52–55, 130–36.

4. Buffalo Jones's life is examined in Robert Easton and MacKenzie Brown, *Lord of Beasts: The Saga of Buffalo Jones* (Tucson: University of Arizona Press, 1961).

5. Grey, "My Own Life," 2–4.

6. Grey, "The Man Who Influenced Me Most," 52–55.

7. Grey to Daniel Murphy, 2 June 1907, Edward Markham Collection, Horrman Library, Wagner College.

8. Ibid.

9. This trip was fictionalized in Grey, *Last of the Plainsmen* (1908).

10. Grey to Murphy, 2 June 1907, Markham Collection.

11. Grey to Mrs. Ripley Hitchcock, 18 September 1918, Ripley Hitchcock Papers, Rare Book and Manuscript Library, Columbia University.

12. Grey to Lina Elise (Dolly) Grey, 20 April 1908, Collection of Zane Grey Incorporated; Grey to David Dexter Rust, 4 March 1908, David Dexter Rust Collection, Church of Jesus Christ of Latter-Day Saints Historical Department; Grey, "Roping Lions in the Grand Canyon," in *Tales of the Lonely Trails* (New York: Harper and Brothers, 1922).

13. Grey to Rust, 4 December 1910 and 2 January 1911, Rust Collection.

14. Ibid., 2 January 1911.

15. Grey to Rust, 14 April 1911, Rust Collection; "Popular Author Visits Flagstaff," *The Coconino Sun* (Flagstaff, Arizona) 21 April 1911, p. 1, col. 5.

16. Grey to Robert Hobart Davis, 29 June 1913, Robert Hobart Davis Papers, Rare Books and Manuscripts Division, The New York Public Library, Astor, Lenox and Tilden Foundations.

17. Dolly Grey to Grey, 26 September 1916, Collection of Zane Grey Incorporated; "Noted Author in Flagstaff," *The Coconino Sun,* 10 September 1915, p. 1, col. 6; "Zane Grey, Famous Author, Here with Party Sunday," *The Coconino Sun,* 29 September 1916, p. 1, col. 4.

18. "Evident Deer Hunt Will Soon Resume and That McCormick's Deer Drive Will

Get Lasky Money," *The Coconino Sun,* 28 November 1924, p. 1, col. 1.

19. "Last Bar Removed; Small Army Now is Bivouacked North of Grand Canyon to Begin Big Deer Drive," *The Coconino Sun,* 12 December 1924, p. 1, col. 5.

20. "Evident Hunt Will Resume," *The Coconino Sun,* 28 November 1924.

21. "Zane Grey Tells Why Drive Failed," *The Coconino Sun,* 19 December 1924, p. 1, col. 1.

22. "Zane Grey Got Only One Bear," *The Coconino Sun,* 4 November 1921, p. 1, col. 3.

CHAPTER II: THE RESERVATION

1. David Lavender, *The Southwest* (New York: Harper and Row, 1980), 175–81. The confinements were ordered by Col. James H. Carleton, commander of the California Column, who occupied New Mexico with Union forces. Carleton, in removing warlike tribes from their native land to reservations, wished to accomplish several goals: secure peace for settlers who were being encouraged to come to New Mexico; gain personal acclaim in his military career; and, ostensibly, protect the Indians.

2. Ruth Underhill, *The Navajos* (Norman: University of Oklahoma Press, 1956), 177–79.

3. Ibid., 164–65.

4. Grey to Rust, 4 December 1910, Rust Collection.

5. Easton and Brown, *Lord of Beasts,* 161–63.

6. Grey to Rust, 26 March 1911, Rust Collection.

7. Grey to Rust, 20 April 1911, Rust Collection.

8. "Allen Doyle, Noted Pioneer and Guide, Died on Monday," *The Coconino Sun,* 11 November 1911, p. 1, col. 6.

9. Mary Appoline Comfort, *Rainbow to Yesterday: The John and Louisa Wetherill Story* (New York: Vantage Press, 1980).

10. Loren Grey to the author, 21 April 1982.

11. Grey, "Nonnezoshe," in *Tales of the Lonely Trails* (New York: Harper and Brothers, 1922), 3. Grey altered the spelling from *Nonnesochie.*

12. Neil M. Judd, "The Discovery of the Rainbow Bridge," in *The Discovery of Rainbow Bridge, the Natural Bridges of Utah, and the Discovery of Betatakin,* Cummings Publication Council Bulletin no. 1 (Tucson, Arizona: The Cummings Publication Council, 1959), 8–13.

13. "Famous Author Makes Trip with Famous Guide," *The Coconino Sun,* 30 May 1913, p. 1, col. 3; Comfort, *Rainbow to Yesterday,* 62–68.

14. Loren Grey, telephone conversation with author, 12 January 1984.

15. Romer C. Grey to Dolly Grey, 14 September 1919, Collection of Zane Grey Incorporated.

16. Grey to Dolly Grey, 21 October 1919, Collection of Zane Grey Incorporated.

17. Dolly Grey to Grey, 22 October 1921, Collection of Zane Grey Incorporated.

18. Dolly's role in the management of Grey's finances can be garnered from her correspondence with her husband; Gruber, *Zane Grey;* Robert Hobart Davis to Grey, 28 March 1916, Davis Papers.

19. "Famous Author Makes Trip," *The Coconino Sun,* 30 May 1913.

20. Ibid.

21. Grey, *The Vanishing American* (1925; reprint, New York: Simon and Schuster, Pocket Books, 1982); Grey, "Blue Feather," in *The Secret of Quaking-Asp Cabin and Other Stories* (New York: Simon and Schuster, Pocket Books, 1983).

22. Grey to Robert Hobart Davis, 29 June 1914, Davis Papers.

23. "Grey Takes Mrs. Robertson to Illustrate Novel," *The Coconino Sun,* 7 April 1922, p. 1, col. 6.

24. "Filming of Famous Grey Novels to Carry Fame of Our Scenery Over World," *The Coconino Sun,* 14 September 1923, p. 1, col. 5.

CHAPTER III: THE DESERT

1. Carey McWillaims, *North from Mexico: The Spanish-Speaking People of the United States* (New York: Greenwood Press, 1968), 57–59.

2. Information on the Mexican Revolution in this and the following paragraph was drawn from Charles C. Cumberland, *Mexican Revolution: Genesis Under Madero* (New York: Greenwood Press, 1952); idem, *Mexican Revolution: The Constitutionalist Years* (Austin: University of Texas Press, 1972); Henry Bamford Parkes, *A History of Mexico* (Boston: Houghton Mifflin, 1969); Rodman Selden, *A Short History of Mexico* (New York: Stein and Day, 1982).

3. Lavender, *The Southwest,* 295.

4. Grey to Robert Hobart Davis, 19 March 1912, Davis Papers.

5. This attitude is very apparent in the book *Desert Gold* (1913).

6. Loren Grey, interview with author, 5 January 1982.

7. Parkes, *A History of Mexico,* 296.

8. Grey, "What the Desert Means to Me," *American Magazine,* November 1924, 5–6.

9. Grey to B. B. Hampton, 2 May 1919, Thomas Nelson Page Papers, William R. Perkins Library, Duke University.

CHAPTER IV: THE FOREST

1. Herbert Eugene Bolton, *Coronado: Knight of Pueblos and Plains* (Albuquerque: University of New Mexico Press, 1949), 107–11.

2. Jack D. Forbes, *Apache, Navajo and Spaniard* (Norman: University of Oklahoma Press, 1960), xiii–xxv.

3. Dan L. Thrapp, *The Conquest of Apacheria* (Norman: University of Oklahoma Press, 1967), 119–37, 217–30, 252–66.

4. Myrtle Haught Branstetter, *Pioneer Hunters of the Rim* (Mesa, Ariz.: Norm's Publishing House, n.d.), 5.

5. Ibid., 33–36.

6. Earle R. Forrest, *Arizona's Dark and Bloody Ground* (London: Andrew Melrose Limited, 1953), 17–31.

7. Lavender, *The Southwest,* 220.

8. Platt Cline, *They Came to the Mountain* (Flagstaff, Ariz.: Northland Press, 1976), 219–20.

9. Clara T. Woody and Milton L. Schwartz, "War in Pleasant Valley: The Outbreak of the Graham-Tewksbury Feud," *Journal of Arizona History* 18, Spring 1977, 44–45.

10. Ibid., 55–56.

11. Grey refers to his initial interest in the Pleasant Valley War in the foreword of *To*

the Last Man (1922; reprint, New York: Simon and Schuster, Pocket Books, 1976).

12. "Zane Grey, Author, Visits Flagstaff," *The Coconino Sun,* 17 September 1918, p. 1, col. 4.

13. Grey to Dolly Grey, 6 October 1919, Collection of Zane Grey Incorporated.

14. See the foreword of *To the Last Man* for a discussion of Grey's experiences in tracking down the origins of the feud.

15. Margaret Sell (proprietor of the Zane Grey cabin), interview with author, Payson, Ariz., 3 April 1982.

16. Ibid.

17. Grey's reaction to Doyle's death was recorded in "Zane Grey Got Only One Bear," *The Coconino Sun,* 4 November 1921, p. 1, col. 3; "Allen Doyle, Noted Pioneer and Guide, Died on Monday," *The Coconino Sun,* 11 November 1921, p. 1, col. 6.

18. "Zane Grey Misses Click of Cowboys' Boots and the Jingle of Their Spurs," *The Coconino Sun,* 25 November 1927, p. 1, col. 3.

19. Cline, *They Came to the Mountain,* 101.

20. Zane Grey's arrival in the vicinity was always newsworthy. "Zane Grey Here Again," *The Coconino Sun,* 29 September 1922, p. 1, col. 6.

21. "Hotel Vital Need of Flag, Says Author Zane Grey," *The Coconino Sun,* 12 October 1923, p. 1, col. 1.

22. "Zane Grey, Here to Hunt and Film Latest Story, Says We've Sure Grown," *The Coconino Sun,* 30 September 1927, p. 1, col. 1.

23. "Zane Grey, Famous Author of Westerns, Here with Party," *The Coconino Sun,* 20 September 1929, p. 1, col. 2.

24. Ibid.

25. For an account of this controversy, see G. M. Farley, "Zane Grey's Fight with Arizona," *The Zane Grey Collector* 4, May 1971, 7–8; *The Coconino Sun:* "Zane Grey Party is Touring the North," 20 August 1929, p. 1, col. 2; "Zane Grey, Famous Author of Westerns, Here with Party," 20 September 1929, p. 1, col. 2; "Zane Grey Says He Will Never Again Visit this State or Write About It," 10 October 1930, p. 1, col. 5.

CHAPTER V: SAGAS OF CANYON COUNTRY

1. Grey, *The Last of the Plainsmen,* 287.

2. Grey, "Don, the Story of a Lion Dog," in *Zane Grey, Outdoorsman,* ed. George Reiger (Englewood Cliffs, N.J.: Prentice-Hall, 1972), 102.

3. Grey to Murphy, 2 June 1907, Markham Collection.

4. Grey, "Roping Lions in the Grand Canyon," in *Zane Grey, Outdoorsman,* 43.

5. Ibid., 47–48.

6. Grey, "Colorado Trails," in *Zane Grey, Outdoorsman,* 217.

7. Grey, "The Man Who Influenced Me Most," 135–36.

8. Ibid., 136.

9. J. Frank Dobie to Grey, 27 March 1924, J. Frank Dobie Collection, The Harry Ransom Humanities Research Center, The University of Texas at Austin.

10. Ibid., 14 May 1924.

11. Ibid., 29 April 1924.

12. Grey, "The Man Who Influenced Me Most," 136.

13. This name actually referred to a location several miles upriver from Lee's Ferry,

where the Domínguez-Escalante expedition of 1776 forded the Colorado River. Frank Waters, *The Colorado* (New York: Holt, Rinehart, and Winston, 1946), 162.

14. Grey, *The Heritage of the Desert* (1910; reprint, New York: Simon and Schuster, Pocket Books, 1968), 35.

15. Grey, "The Man Who Influenced Me Most," 53.

16. Grey, *The Heritage of the Desert*, 41–42.

17. Grey, "The Man Who Influenced Me Most," 52, 54.

18. Grey to Rust, 2 January 1911, Rust Collection.

19. Grey, *The Heritage of the Desert*, 210.

20. *Riders of the Purple Sage* was ahead of its time; this reversal of traditional values is more often found in westerns of the 1960s. John Cawelti, "God's Country, Las Vegas, and the Gunfighter," *Western American Literature* 9 February 1975, 273–83.

21. Grey, *Riders of the Purple Sage* (1912; reprint, New York: Simon and Schuster, Pocket Books, 1980), 12.

22. Ibid., 13.

23. Grey to Rust, 4 December 1910, Rust Collection.

24. Polygamy was abolished by the Mormon church in 1890. Robert V. Hine, *The American West: An Interpretive History* (Boston: Little, Brown, 1973), 231.

25. Grey, *The Rainbow Trail* (1915; reprint, New York: Simon and Schuster, Pocket Books, 1961), 64.

26. Mention of Grey's female traveling companions is first found in "Noted Author in Flagstaff," *The Coconino Sun*, 10 September 1915, p. 1, col. 8.

27. Leonard Arrington and Jon Haupt, "Community and Isolation: Some Aspects of 'Mormon Westerns,' " *Western American Literature* 8, Spring/Summer 1973, 18–20.

28. Grey, *The Rainbow Trail*, 110.

29. Ibid., 75–76.

30. Grey to Dolly Grey, 21 October 1919, Collection of Zane Grey Incorporated.

31. Grey, *The Deer Stalker* (1949; reprint, New York: Simon and Schuster, Pocket Books, 1965), 45–46.

32. This river plays a prominent role in *The Last of the Plainsmen, Heritage of the Desert, Wildfire, The Deer Stalker, Stranger from the Tonto, Boulder Dam, Roping Lions in the Grand Canyon,* "Don, the Story of a Lion Dog," and "The Man Who Influenced Me Most."

33. "Zane Grey Visits Boulder on Sunday," *The Las Vegas Evening Review-Journal* (Las Vegas, Nevada) 20 November 1933, p. 4, col. 2.

34. Loren Grey, interview with author, 5 January 1982. This novel, although not set in Arizona, is appropriate for inclusion here because of the prominence the Colorado River had in it and because, between 1863 and 1867, the southern tip of Nevada was part of the Arizona Territory.

35. Grey, *Boulder Dam* (1900; reprint, New York: Simon and Schuster, Pocket Books, 1970), 2.

CHAPTER VI: THE RESERVATION BOOKS

1. Grey to Al Doyle, 16 January 1918, in *The Coconino Sun*, 1 March 1918, p. 1, col. 4.

2. Grey, *The Vanishing American,* 137.

3. Another novel in which the theme of disappearing Indian culture was introduced is *The Rainbow Trail* (1915), considered with the Arizona Strip novels *(Sagas of Canyon Country).* Grey's strong statements leave no doubt about his conviction that the Indian was a dying breed.

4. Grey, *The Vanishing American,* 311.

5. Ibid., 116.

6. Ibid., 139.

7. Grey to *Ladies Home Journal,* 30 June 1922.

8. Loren Grey, in his foreword to the reprint edition of *The Vanishing American,* notes the omission of this material in the original edition; he restored it to the 1982 reprint. The marriage of Nophaie and Marian Warner is less shocking now, and provides a symbolic expression of the solution to the "Indian question" as perceived by Zane Grey.

9. Grey, *The Vanishing American,* 116.

10. Ibid., 190.

11. Information on the serialization of Grey's novels was drawn from Frank Gruber's chapters entitled "The Books," and "The Magazine Stories," 232–47. *Captives of the Desert* was published as a book in 1952.

12. Grey, *The Vanishing American,* 100.

13. Grey, *Wild Horse Mesa* (1928; reprint, New York: Simon and Schuster, Pocket Books, 1983), 23.

14. Grey, *Captives of the Desert* (1952; reprint, New York: Simon and Schuster, Pocket Books, 1977), 101.

15. Grey, *The Vanishing American,* 156.

16. Ibid., 189.

17. Dolly Grey to Alvah James, 22 March 1953, Collection of Zane Grey Home. The same idea was stated by Loren Grey in his foreword to *The Vanishing American.*

18. Grey, *The Vanishing American,* 139.

19. Grey, *The Rainbow Trail,* 97.

20. Grey, *The Vanishing American,* 103, 339–40.

21. These attitudes are demonstrated in *Riders of the Purple Sage* (1912) and *The Rainbow Trail* (1915).

22. Grey to William Briggs and Henry Hoyns, 25 May 1925, included in Loren Grey's foreword to reprint edition of *The Vanishing American.*

23. Grey, *The Vanishing American,* 142.

24. Ibid., 155.

25. Ibid., 158–59.

26. Ibid., 156.

27. Ibid., 157.

28. Ibid., 170.

29. According to Loren Grey in the book's foreword, the circumstances described were based upon events that occurred on the reservation before and during World War I. "The historical data behind these revelations were accurate, despite the emotionalism

with which they were often presented."

30. Frank McNitt, *The Indian Traders* (Norman: University of Oklahoma Press, 1962), 68–86.

31. Loren Grey to author, 21 April 1982.

32. Ibid.

33. Ibid.

34. Grey, *The Rainbow Trail*, 30–31.

35. Grey, "What the Desert Means to Me"; *The Rainbow Trail*, 220–21; "Nonnezoshe–The Rainbow Bridge," *Recreation Magazine*, 1915.

36. Ibid.

37. Loren Grey, interview with author, 5 January 1982.

CHAPTER VII: STORIES OF THE BORDER

1. Grey to Robert Hobart Davis, 19 March 1912, Davis Papers.

2. Grey, *Desert Gold* (1913; reprint, New York: Simon and Schuster, Pocket Books, 1969), 72.

3. Ibid., 28.

4. Grey, *The Light of Western Stars* (1914; reprint, New York: Simon and Schuster, Pocket Books, 1962), 306.

5. Ibid., 61.

6. Grey, *Desert Gold*, 100.

7. Ibid., 101.

8. Grey, *The Light of Western Stars*, 57.

9. Grey, "What the Desert Means to Me." Ever curious, Grey and a close friend, Sievert Nielson, hiked across Death Valley in January 1919. This excursion confirmed Grey's suppositions about the thoughts and feelings of men who spent their lives in this environment (Frank Gruber, *Zane Grey*, 129–34).

10. Grey, *Stranger from the Tonto* (1956; reprint, New York: Simon and Schuster, Pocket Books, 1964), 14.

11. Grey, *Desert Gold*, 225–26.

12. Grey, "What the Desert Means to Me."

13. Grey, "Amber's Mirage," in *Amber's Mirage and Other Stories* (New York: Simon and Schuster, Pocket Books, 1983), 28.

14. Grey, *Desert Gold*, 6–7.

CHAPTER VIII: TALES OF THE TONTO

1. Grey to Dolly Grey, 6 October 1919, Collection of Zane Grey Incorporated.

2. Clara T. Woody and Milton L. Schwartz, *Globe, Arizona: Early Times in a Little World of Copper and Cattle.* (Tucson: Arizona Historical Society, 1977), 101–2. With some modifications, Grey included one of the more macabre episodes of the feud: the Graham attack of the Tewksbury's cabin on 2 September 1887, in which two of the latter were surprised and killed and the cabin's inhabitants were besieged for several days, unable to recover the bodies of the dead men that were, by the end of the siege, very attractive to flies and hogs.

3. Lavender, *The Southwest*, 218–19.

4. Ibid.

5. Woody and Schwartz, *Globe, Arizona*, 124.

6. Grey, *The Hash Knife Outfit* (1934; reprint, New York: Simon and Schuster, Pocket Books, 1975), 9.

7. Grey's research into the Graham-Tewksbury feud led him to investigate other southwestern range wars, particularly New Mexico's Lincoln County War. References to this conflict appear in one of the Tonto Basin novels, *Shadow on the Trail* (1946).

8. Grey, *Arizona Clan* (1958; reprint, New York: Simon and Schuster, Pocket Books, 1966), 32.

9. Grey, *Stranger from the Tonto*, 149.

10. Grey, "The Saga of the Ice Cream Kid," in *Amber's Mirage and Other Stories*, 163–81.

11. Grey, *Shadow on the Trail* (1946; reprint, New York: Simon and Schuster, Pocket Books, 1970), 77.

12. Grey used the cowboys' life as the subject of several short stories, some of which had a humorous twist. In "The Flight of Fargo Jones," a cowboy who escapes hanging breaks the handcuffs to free himself; when recaptured, he is told that he has been cleared of all charges except the destruction of the handcuffs. "The Camp Robber" is a more serious story about a cowboy accused of stealing the ranch's payroll; this story is set in the Clear Creek–Cottonwood–Verde River locale.

13. "Lasky Film Company Finish Filming Grey's 'Sunset Pass,' " The Coconino Sun, 16 November 1928, p. 1, col. 5.

14. Grey, *Sunset Pass* (1931; reprint, New York: Simon and Schuster, Pocket Books, 1975), 104–5.

15. Loren Grey, foreword to *30,000 on the Hoof* (1940; reprint, New York: Simon and Schuster, Pocket Books, 1982), 5–6.

16. Because the subject of rape, particularly of a white woman by an Indian, was unacceptable to Grey's readers when the book was first published in 1940, the episode was omitted, not to be restored until the 1982 reprinting at Loren Grey's request. Dr. Grey is concerned that his father's novels be available in the form in which they were written. Loren Grey, interview with author, 5 January 1982.

17. Grey, *Code of the West* (1934; reprint, New York: Simon and Schuster, Pocket Books, 1963), 1.

18. Ibid., 220.

19. Ibid., 4.

20. Joseph Stocker, "Zane Grey and Pleasant Valley," *Westways*, February 1960, 30–31; Branstetter, *Pioneer Hunters*, 82–83.

21. Grey, *Man of the Forest* (1920; reprint, New York: Simon and Schuster, Pocket Books, 1977), 109.

22. Ibid., 132.

23. Ibid., 136.

24. Grey's accounts appear in *The Country Gentleman* 18 December 1920, 3 March 1923, and 8 March 1924.

25. Grey, "Arizona Bear," *The Country Gentleman*, 18 December 1920.

26. Ibid.

CHAPTER IX: ZANE GREY AND THE FILM INDUSTRY

1. Kenneth W. Leish, *Cinema* (New York: Newsweek Books, 1974), 7–11.

2. Carlton Jackson, *Zane Grey,* 13.

3. Leish, *Cinema,* 12–17.

4. William K. Everson, *A Pictorial History of the Western Film* (Secaucus, N.J.: Citadel Press, 1969), 14–15.

5. Thomas Schatz, *Hollywood Genres: Formulas, Filmmaking, and the Studio System* (Philadelphia: Temple University Press, 1981), 46.

6. Gruber, *Zane Grey,* 127.

7. "Zane Grey's 'Wanderer of the Wasteland': Our Beautiful Painted Desert of Arizona Made in Natural Colors," *The Coconino Sun,* 24 December 1924, p. 12, col. 5.

8. Information on the titles, dates of release, characters, and actors, unless otherwise stated, is from Kenneth W. Scott, *Zane Grey: Born to the West* (Boston: G. K. Hall and Co., 1979).

9. *The Coconino Sun,* as always, followed Grey's activities closely: "Zane Grey, Noted Author, to Make Movies on the Painted Desert," 18 February 1916, p. 1, col. 4; "L.A. Movie Company Will Film Zane Grey's Famous Books Here," 1 March 1918, p. 1, col. 4; "Farnum, the Famous Movie Star, is Here," 17 May 1918, p. 1, col. 8. The Fox Studios also created their own publicity materials. As Scott discusses in *Zane Grey: Born to the West,* an 11 May 1918 telegram from Grey was quoted in which he explained the Mormon practice of sealed wives. This involvement presumably ensured the veracity of the Fox–Zane Grey films.

10. Robert Hobart Davis to Grey, 28 March 1916, Davis Papers.

11. Jon Tuska, *The Filming of the West* (Garden City, N.Y.: Doubleday, 1976), 123.

12. Gruber, *Zane Grey,* 128–29.

13. Grey to Benjamin H. Hampton, 1 May 1919, Page Papers.

14. Ibid.

15. Grey, "On Location," in *The Camp Robber and Other Stories* (Roslyn, N.Y.: Walter J. Black Inc., 1979), 77–115.

16. Zane Grey Productions also made three non-Arizona films: *Riders of the Dawn* (1920), based on *The Desert of Wheat* and set in the state of Washington; *The Mysterious Rider* (1921), from the novel of the same name; and *Golden Dreams* (1922), based on a short story.

17. Gruber, *Zane Grey,* 192; Tuska, *The Filming of the West,* 123.

18. For an autobiographical account of the early years of filmmaking, see Jesse L. Lasky with Don Weldon, *I Blow My Own Horn* (Garden City, N.Y: Doubleday, 1957).

19. Gruber, *Zane Grey,* 196; Tuska, *The Filming of the West,* 131.

20. "Filming of Famous Grey Novels to Carry Fame of Our Scenery Over World," *The Coconino Sun,* 14 September 1923, p. 1, col. 7.

21. Gruber, *Zane Grey,* 126–27; Tuska, *The Filming of the West,* 124, 131.

22. Grey to Dolly Grey, 12 June 1923, Collection of Zane Grey Incorporated.

23. Branstetter, *Pioneer Hunters of the Rim,* 82.

24. "Famous Screen Stars Here in Three Weeks to Film Grey Novel," *The Coconino*

Sun, 10 August 1923, p. 1, col. 1.

25. "Flagstaff Enjoying New Lasky Picture Before It's Produced," *The Coconino Sun,* 7 September 1923, p. 1, col. 3; "Indians Are Rounding Up Equines for Grey Movies," *The Coconino Sun,* 12 October 1923, p. 1, col. 8.

26. "Flagstaff Enjoying New Lasky Picture," *The Coconino Sun,* 7 September 1923, p. 1, col. 3; "Moving Picture Work Slowed Up by Rain," *The Coconino Sun,* 21 September 1923, p. 1, col. 1.

27. "Filming of Famous Grey Novels," *The Coconino Sun,* 14 September 1923.

28. Ibid., "Indians are Rounding Up Equines," *The Coconino Sun,* 12 October 1923; "Bebe Daniels, Picture Star, Here; Others Soon Coming," *The Coconino Sun,* 5 October 1923, p. 1, col. 1.

29. "Indians are Rounding Up Equines," *The Coconino Sun,* 12 October 1923; "Bebe Daniels, Picture Star, Here," *The Coconino Sun,* 5 October 1923; "Hotel Vital Need of Flag," *The Coconino Sun,* 12 October 1923; Scott, *Zane Grey,* 8.

30. "Hotel Vital Need of Flag," *The Coconino Sun,* 12 October 1923.

31. Robert Hobart Davis to Grey, 28 March 1916, Davis Papers; Gruber, *Zane Grey,* 126; Tuska, *The Filming of the West,* 123.

32. Tom Mix, a native of Pennsylvania, had a taste for adventure; he saw military action in Cuba, the Philippines, China, and South Africa between 1898 and 1902. When he returned to the United States, he found employment as a trick rider with an Oklahoma-based "Wild West" show (he developed a close friendship with Will Rogers during this period). In 1910, a movie company came to the Oklahoma ranch to film a documentary, and Mix got a chance to perform for the camera. Thereafter, he was in a number of films, and found time as well to travel to Canada and Mexico; while in Mexico, he fought on Madero's side of the revolution. In 1917, he joined Fox Studios and quickly rose to stardom in their western films. For more information, see John H. Nicholas, *Tom Mix: Riding to Glory* (Kansas City, Mo.: The Lowell Press, A Persimmon Hill Book, 1980).

33. *The Coconino Sun* followed closely the complexities of this planning: "Noted Film Directors Here Hunting Locations for Filming Zane Grey's 'Vanishing American,' " 25 July 1924, p. 1, col. 7; " 'Vanishing American' Soon to be Filmed; We Owe Much to Zane Grey," 8 August 1924, p. 1, col. 8; " 'Vanishing American' Filming is Postponed," 22 August 1924, p. 1, col. 3; "Movie People Here to Film Zane Grey's 'White Horse Mesa,' " 24 April 1925, p. 1, col. 8; and " 'Vanishing American' Outfitting Here, to be Filmed Early in June," 22 May 1925, p. 1, col. 8.

34. Ibid., all.

35. Scott, *Zane Grey,* 9.

36. Branstetter, *Pioneer Hunters of the Rim,* 82.

37. *The Coconino Sun:* " 'Vanishing American' Outfitting Here," 22 May 1925; "Now Filming Zane Grey's 'Vanishing American,' " 3 July 1925, p. 1, col. 4; "Over 3500 Indians Ready for Grey's Big Picture," 31 July 1925, p. 1, col. 4; Scott, *Zane Grey,* 10.

38. Paramount made five more movies based on Grey's novels in 1926 and 1927; none of them were filmed in Arizona, however. They were: *Desert Gold* (1926), George B. Seitz, director; *Born to the West* (1926) starred Jack Holt as Dare "Colorado" Rudd and Raymond Hatton as Jim Fallon; *Man of the Forest* (1926) again featuring Jack Holt, this time as Milt Dale (the title role) and Warner Oland as the treacherous outlaw, Beas-

ley; *Nevada* (1927), featuring a young actor new to motion-picture audiences—Gary Cooper—in the title role; and *Open Range* (1927) based on *Valley of Wild Horses.* Tuska, *The Filming of the West,* 120.

39. "Moving Picture Co. Arrives Here; Will Locate at The Gap," *The Coconino Sun,* 25 March 1927, p. 1, col. 5.

40. "Zane Grey, Here to Hunt and Film Latest Story," *The Coconino Sun,* 30 September 1927.

41. "Zane Grey Classifies Hollywood Movies," *The Coconino Sun,* 28 October 1927, sec. 2, p. 1, col. 4.

42. "Zane Grey's 'The Water Hole' Will be Filmed Here Next Month," *The Coconino Sun,* 1 June 1928, p. 1, col. 1.

43. From *The Coconino Sun:* "Zane Grey's 'Avalanche' Will be Filmed Here by Famous Players–Lasky," 10 August 1928, p. 1, col. 1; "Famous Russian Artiste Supporting Jack Holt in 'Avalanche' Filming Here," 7 September 1928, p. 1, col. 7; " 'Avalanche' Picture Company Left Sunday," 14 September 1928, p. 1, col. 7.

44. From *The Coconino Sun:* "Lasky Film Company Finish 'Sunset Pass,' " 16 November 1928; "Movie People Stayed, Filmed Snow Fight," 16 November 1928, p. 1, col. 3.

45. "Zane Grey Classifies Hollywood Movies," *The Coconino Sun,* 28 October 1927.

46. Tuska, *The Filming of the West,* 278; "The American Western Cinema: 1903–Present," in *Focus on the Western,* ed. Jack Nachbar (Englewood Cliffs, N.J.: Prentice-Hall, 1974), 34.

47. Information on names of films and release dates is from Scott, *Zane Grey.*

48. George N. Fenin and William K. Everson, *The Western: From Silents to Cinerama* (New York: Orion Press, 1962), 34.

49. "Zane Grey's 'Lone Star Ranger' to be Filmed Here," *The Coconino Sun,* 26 July 1929.

50. "Zane Grey, Famous Author of Westerns, Here with Party," *The Coconino Sun,* 20 September 1929; "Blooded Horses and Hounds Sent Out for Movie Now Filming," *The Coconino Sun,* 27 September 1929, p. 8, col. 4.

51. From *The Coconino Sun:* "Fox Film Troupe Begins Filming of Zane Grey's 'Riders of the Purple Sage,' " 24 July 1931, p. 1, col. 7; "$50,000 Replica of Mormon Village Swept by Flames as Climax of Movie Production," 7 August 1931, p. 1, col. 1; "Fox 'Rainbow Trail' Film Work at Grand Canyon Nearly Done," 23 October 1931, p. 1, col. 2.

52. " 'Robber's Roost' Film Work Brought 60 Fox People Here Wednesday," *The Coconino Sun,* 23 September 1932, p. 1, col. 1; Scott, *Zane Grey,* 18.

53. Gruber, *Zane Grey,* 192; Tuska, *The Filming of the West,* 326.

54. Fenin and Everson, *The Westerns,* 198; Tuska, *The Filming of the West,* 328.

55. "Buster" Crabbe was an athlete who only accepted roles in which he played characters with sterling qualities: courage, honesty, and superlative physical prowess. He enlivened such roles as Buck Rogers and Flash Gordon; in later films for Producers Releasing Corporation, he consented to play the character of Billy the Kid only after that notorious figure was "transformed into a conventional western hero." Fenin and Everson, *The Westerns,* 243. In the Zane Grey westerns, Crabbe was a traditional Grey hero who was sincere, trustworthy, physically strong, and swashbuckling.

56. Tuska, *The Filming of the West,* 446; Fenin and Everson, *The Westerns,* 255.

57. Information on Harry Sherman's background is from Tuska, *The Filming of the West,* 313–15, 329.

58. Tuska, *The Filming of the West,* 448.

CHAPTER X: THE LEGEND OF ZANE GREY

1. Gruber, *Zane Grey,* 219.

2. Grey to Alvah James, 26 October 1936, Collection of Zane Grey Home.

3. Zane Grey's obituary, *Newsweek,* 30 October 1939, 7.

4. Margaret Sell, interview with author, Payson, Arizona, 3 April 1982.

5. Printing history in *Nevada* (1928; reprint, New York: Bantam Books, 1980).

6. M. Sell, interview with author; Zane Grey obituary, *Publisher's Weekly,* 28 October 1939, 1698; "More to Come," *The New Yorker,* 19 July 1942, 17–18.

7. For a discussion of Grey's treatment of the effects of isolation on Mormon individuals and communities, see Arrington and Haupt, "Community and Isolation," 15–31.

8. Grey, *Black Mesa* (1955; reprint, New York: Simon and Schuster, Pocket Books, 1966), 38.

9. Frantz and Choate, *The American Cowboy,* 173–74.

BIBLIOGRAPHY

PRIMARY SOURCES

BOOKS BY ZANE GREY

Arizona Ames. 1928. Reprint. New York: Simon and Schuster, Pocket Books, 1973.

Arizona Clan. 1958. Reprint. New York: Simon and Schuster, Pocket Books, 1966.

Black Mesa. 1955. Reprint. New York: Simon and Schuster, Pocket Books, 1966.

Boulder Dam. 1933. Reprint. New York: Simon and Schuster, Pocket Books, 1960.

Call of the Canyon. 1924. Reprint. New York: Simon and Schuster, Pocket Books, 1975.

Captives of the Desert. New York: Simon and Schuster, Pocket Books, 1977.

Code of the West. 1934. Reprint. New York: Simon and Schuster, Pocket Books, 1963.

The Deer Stalker. 1949. Reprint. New York: Simon and Schuster, Pocket Books, 1965.

Desert Gold. 1913. Reprint. New York: Simon and Schuster, Pocket Books, 1969.

Drift Fence. 1913. Reprint. New York: Simon and Schuster, Pocket Books, 1957.

The Dude Ranger. 1951. Reprint. New York: Simon and Schuster, Pocket Books, 1981.

Forlorn River. 1926. Reprint. New York: Simon and Schuster, Pocket Books, 1974.

The Hash Knife Outfit. 1934. Reprint. New York: Simon and Schuster, Pocket Books, 1975.

The Heritage of the Desert. 1910. Reprint. New York: Simon and Schuster, Pocket Books, 1968.

Knights of the Range. 1936. Reprint. New York: Simon and Schuster, Pocket Books, 1961.

The Last of the Plainsmen. 1908. Reprint. Roslyn, New York: Walter J. Black, Inc., n.d.

The Light of Western Stars. 1914. Reprint. New York: Simon and Schuster, Pocket Books, 1962.

Lone Star Ranger. 1915. Reprint. New York: Simon and Schuster, Pocket Books, 1969.

Lost Pueblo. 1954. Reprint. New York: Simon and Schuster, Pocket Books, 1965.

Majesty's Rancho. 1937. Reprint. New York: Simon and Schuster, Pocket Books, 1980.

Man of the Forest. 1920. Reprint. New York: Simon and Schuster, Pocket Books, 1977.

The Mysterious Rider. 1921. Reprint. New York: Simon and Schuster, Pocket Books, 1969.

Nevada. 1928. Reprint. New York: Bantam Books, 1946.

Raiders of Spanish Peaks. 1931. Reprint. New York: Simon and Schuster, Pocket Books, 1960.

The Rainbow Trail. 1915. Reprint. New York: Simon and Schuster, Pocket Books, 1961.

Riders of the Purple Sage. 1912. Reprint. New York: Simon and Schuster, Pocket Books, 1980.

Robber's Roost. 1930. Reprint. New York: Simon and Schuster, Pocket Books, 1969.

Roping Lions in the Grand Canyon. 1924. Reprinted in *Zane Grey: Outdoorsman*. Edited by George Reiger. Englewood Cliffs, N.J.: Prentice-Hall, 1972.

Shadow on the Trail. 1946. Reprint. New York: Simon and Schuster, Pocket Books, 1970.

Stairs of Sand. 1928. Reprint. New York: Simon and Schuster, Pocket Books, 1981.

Stranger from the Tonto. 1956. Reprint. New York: Simon and Schuster, Pocket Books, 1964.

Sunset Pass. 1931. Reprint. New York: Simon and Schuster, Pocket Books, 1975.

30,000 on the Hoof. 1940. Reprint. New York: Simon and Schuster, Pocket Books, 1982.

The Thundering Herd. 1925. Reprint. New York: Simon and Schuster, Pocket Books, 1983.

To the Last Man. 1922. Reprint. New York: Simon and Schuster, Pocket Books, 1976.

Under the Tonto Rim. 1926. Reprint. New York: Simon and Schuster, Pocket Books, 1976.

The U.P. Trail. 1918. Reprint. New York: Simon and Schuster, Pocket Books, 1956.

The Vanishing American. 1925. Reprint. New York: Simon and Schuster, Pocket Books, 1982.

Wildfire. 1917. Reprint. London: White Lion, 1974.

Wild Horse Mesa. 1928. Reprint. New York: Simon and Schuster, Pocket Books, 1983.

The Young Forester. 1910. Reprint. New York: Grosset and Dunlap, 1938.

SHORT STORIES BY ZANE GREY

"Amber's Mirage." In *Amber's Mirage and Other Stories*. New York: Simon and Schuster, Pocket Books, 1983.

"Blue Feather." In *The Secret of Quaking-Asp Cabin and Other Stories*. New York:

Simon and Schuster, Pocket Books, 1983.

"Canyon Walls." In *The Western Story: Fact, Fiction, and Myth*. Edited by Philip Durham and Evertt L. Jones. New York: Harcourt, Brace, and Jovanovich, 1975.

"Don, the Story of a Lion Dog." In *Amber's Mirage and Other Stories*. New York: Simon and Schuster, Pocket Books, 1983.

"Fantoms of Peace." In *Amber's Mirage and Other Stories*. New York: Simon and Schuster, Pocket Books, 1983.

"Lightning." In *The Secret of Quaking-Asp Cabin and Other Stories*. New York: Simon and Schuster, Pocket Books, 1983.

"Monty Price's Nightingale." In *The Secret of Quaking-Asp Cabin and Other Stories*. New York: Simon and Schuster, Pocket Books, 1983.

"On Location." In *The Camp Robber and Other Stories*. Roslyn, New York: Walter J. Black, Inc., 1979.

"Tappan's Burro." In *Tappan's Burro and Other Stories*. New York: Simon and Schuster, Pocket Books, 1982.

"The Camp Robber." In *The Camp Robber and Other Stories*. Roslyn, New York: Walter J. Black, Inc., 1979.

"The Flight of Fargo Jones." In *The Secret of Quaking-Asp Cabin and Other Stories*. New York: Simon and Schuster, Pocket Books, 1983.

"The Kidnapping of Collie Younger." In *The Wolf Tracker and Other Stories*. Roslyn, New York: Walter J. Black, Inc., 1976.

"The Saga of the Ice Cream Kid." In *Amber's Mirage and Other Stories*. New York: Simon and Schuster, Pocket Books, 1983.

"The Secret of Quaking-Asp Cabin." In *The Secret of Quaking-Asp Cabin and Other Stories*. New York: Simon and Schuster, Pocket Books, 1983.

"The Wolf Tracker." In *The Wolf Tracker and Other Stories*. Roslyn, New York: Walter J. Black, Inc., 1951.

"Yaqui." In *Tappan's Burro and Other Stories*. New York: Simon and Schuster, Pocket Books, 1982.

ARTICLES BY ZANE GREY

"Arizona Bear." *The Country Gentleman*, 11 December 1920.

"Arizona Bear." *The Country Gentleman*, 18 December 1920.

"Bear Trails." *The Country Gentleman*, 3 March 1923.

"Bear Trails." *The Country Gentleman*, 10 March 1923.

"Bear Trails." *The Country Gentleman*, 17 March 1923.

"Colorado Trails." In *Zane Grey: Outdoorsman*. Edited by George Reiger. Englewood Cliffs, N.J.: Prentice-Hall, 1972.

"Death Valley." *Harpers*, May 1920.

"Down Into the Desert." *Ladies Home Journal*, January 1924.

"Keys to Greatness." *Coronet*, May 1951.

"My Own Life." In *Zane Grey: The Man and His Work*. New York: Harper and Brothers, 1928.

"Nonnezoshe, the Rainbow Bridge." In *Zane Grey: Outdoorsman*. Edited by George Reiger. Englewood Cliffs, N.J.: Prentice-Hall, 1972.

"The Living Past." *Zane Grey Collector* 7, no. 2 (1972).

"The Man Who Influenced Me Most." *American Magazine,* August 1926.

"Tonto Basin." In *Zane Grey: Outdoorsman.* Edited by George Reiger. Englewood Cliffs, N.J.: Prentice-Hall, 1972.

"Tonto Bear." *The Country Gentleman,* 8 March 1924.

"What the Desert Means to Me." *American Magazine,* November 1924.

"What the Open Means to Me." In *Zane Grey: The Man and His Work.* New York: Harper and Brothers, 1928.

UNPUBLISHED MATERIAL

Beard, Daniel. *Daniel Beard Papers.* Library of Congress, Washington, D. C.

Davis, Robert Hobart. *Robert Hobart Davis Papers.* New York Public Library, New York City, New York.

Deland, Margaret. *Margaret Deland Collection.* Colby College, Waterville, Maine.

Farley, G. M. *G. M. Farley Collection.* Hagerstown, Maryland.

Garland, Hamlin. *Hamlin Garland Collection.* University of Southern California, Los Angeles, California.

Grey, Zane. *Zane Grey Collection.* Beinecke Rare Book and Manuscript Library, Yale University Library, New Haven, Connecticut.

———. *Zane Grey Collection.* Clifton Waller Barrett Library, University of Virginia, Charlottesville, Virginia.

———. *Zane Grey Collection.* The Elmer Holmes Bobst Library, New York University, New York City, New York.

———. *Zane Grey Collection.* The Harry Ransom Humanities Research Center, University of Texas at Austin, Austin, Texas.

———. *Zane Grey Collection.* Houghton Library, Harvard University, Cambridge, Massachusetts.

———. *Zane Grey Collection.* Los Angeles Public Library, Los Angeles, California.

———. *Zane Grey Collection.* Pierpont Morgan Library, New York City, New York.

———. *Zane Grey Collection.* Zane Grey Home, Lackawaxen, Pennsylvania.

———. *Zane Grey Collection.* Zane Grey Incorporated, Woodland Hills, California.

Hitchcock, Ripley. *Ripley Hitchcock Collection.* Rare Book and Manuscript Library, Columbia University Library, New York City, New York.

Jansen, Roy. *Roy Jansen Collection.* State Library of Pennsylvania, Harrisburg, Pennsylvania.

Markham, Edwin. *Edwin Markham Collection.* Horrman Library, Wagner College, New York City, New York.

Page, Thomas Nelson. *Thomas Nelson Page Papers.* William R. Perkins Library, Duke University Library, Durham, North Carolina.

Parsons, George W. *George W. Parsons Collection.* Arizona Historical Society, Tucson, Arizona.

Rust, David Dexter. *David Dexter Rust Papers.* Church of Jesus Christ of Latter-Day Saints, Historical Department, Salt Lake City, Utah.

NEWSPAPERS

The Coconino Sun, Flagstaff, Arizona, 1911–1932.

Las Vegas Review Journal, Las Vegas, Nevada, 1933.

SECONDARY SOURCES

BOOKS

Berkhofer, Robert F., Jr. *The White Man's Indian: Images of the American Indian from Columbus to the Present.* New York: Random House, 1978.

Branch, Douglas. *The Cowboy and His Interpreters.* New York: Cooper Square Publishers, 1961.

Bolton, Herbert E. *Coronado: Knight of Pueblos and Plains.* Albuquerque: University of New Mexico Press, 1949.

Calder, Jennie. *There Must be a Lone Ranger: The American West in Film and Reality.* London: Hamish Hamilton, 1974.

Cawelti, John. *Adventure, Mystery, and Romance: Formula Stories as Art and Popular Culture.* Chicago: University of Chicago Press, 1976.

————. *The Six-Gun Mystique.* Bowling Green, Ohio: Bowling Green University Popular Press, 1971.

Churchill, Allen. *The Literary Decade.* Englewood Cliffs, New Jersey: Prentice-Hall, 1971.

Comfort, Mary Appoline. *Rainbow to Yesterday: The John and Louisa Wetherill Story.* New York: Vantage Press, 1980.

Cumberland, Charles C. *Mexican Revolution: The Constitutional Years.* Austin: University of Texas Press, 1972.

Dickens, Homer. *The Films of Gary Cooper.* New York: Citadel Press, 1970.

Dobie, J. Frank. *Guide to Life and Literature of the Southwest.* Dallas, Texas: Southern Methodist University Press, 1952.

Dutton, Bertha P. *American Indians of the Southwest.* Albuquerque: University of New Mexico Press, 1983.

Easton, Robert, and Mackenzie Brown. *Lord of Beasts: The Life of Buffalo Jones.* Tucson: University of Arizona Press, 1961.

Everson, William K. *A Pictorial History of the Western Film.* Secaucus, New Jersey: The Citadel Press, 1969.

Fenin, George N., and William K. Everson. *The Western: From Silents to Cinerama.* New York: Orion Press, 1962.

Frantz, Joe B., and Julian Ernest Choate, Jr. *The American Cowboy: The Myth and the Reality.* Norman: University of Oklahoma Press, 1955.

Gay, Carol. *Zane Grey, Story Teller.* Columbus, Ohio: State Library of Ohio, 1979.

Gruber, Frank. *Zane Grey.* New York: Signet, 1971.

Jackson, Carlton. *Zane Grey.* Boston: G. K. Hall and Company, 1973.

Kerr, Jean. *Zane Grey, Man of the West.* New York: Grosset and Dunlap, 1949.

Lasky, Jesse L., with Don Weldon. *I Blow My Own Horn.* Garden City, New York: Doubleday, 1957.

Leish, Kenneth W. *Cinema.* New York: Newsweek Books, 1974.

McNitt, Frank. *The Indian Traders.* Norman: University of Oklahoma Press, 1962.

McWilliams, Carey. *North from Mexico: The Spanish-Speaking People of the United States.* New York: Greenwood Press, 1968.

Nachbar, Jack, ed. *Focus on the Western*. Englewood Cliffs, New Jersey: Prentice-Hall, 1974.

Nash, Roderick. *The Nervous Generation: American Thought, 1917–1930*. Chicago: Rand McNally, 1970.

Nicholas, John H. *Tom Mix: Riding up to Glory*. Kansas City, Missouri: The Lowell Press, A Persimmon Hill Book, 1980.

Noble, David. *The Progressive Mind, 1890–1917*. Chicago: Rand McNally, 1970.

Nye, Russel B. *The Unembarrassed Muse: The Popular Arts in America*. New York: Dial Press, 1970.

Parkes, Henry Bamford. *A History of Mexico*. Boston: Houghton Mifflin Company, 1969.

Reiger, George, ed. *Zane Grey: Outdoorsman*. Englewood Cliffs, N.J.: Prentice-Hall, 1972.

Ronald, Ann. *Zane Grey*. Boise, Idaho: Boise State University Press, 1975.

Rusho, W. L., and Gregory C. Crampton. *Desert River Crossing: Historic Lee's Ferry on the Colorado River*. Santa Barbara, California: Peregrine-Smith, 1981.

Schatz, Thomas. *Hollywood Genres: Formulas, Filmmaking, and the Studio System*. Philadelphia: Temple University Press, 1981.

Schneider, Norris F. *Zane Grey: The Man Whose Books Made the West Famous*. Zanesville, Ohio: Norris F. Schneider, 1967.

Scott, Kenneth William. *Zane Grey: Born to the West*. Boston: G. K. Hall, 1979.

Selden, Rodman. *A Short History of Mexico*. New York: Stein and Day, Publishers, 1982.

Smith, Henry Nash. *Virgin Land: The American West as Symbol and Myth*. New York: Vintage Books, 1957.

Tuska, Jon. *The Filming of the West*. Garden City, New York: Doubleday, 1976.

Womack, John Jr. *Zapata and the Mexican Revolution*. New York: Alfred A. Knopf, 1971.

Woody, Clara T., and Milton J. Schwartz. *Globe, Arizona: Early Times in a Little World of Copper and Cattle*. Tucson: Arizona Historical Society, 1977.

Zane Grey: The Man and His Work. New York: Harper and Brothers, 1928.

ARTICLES

Arrington, Leonard, and Jon Haupt. "Community and Isolation: Some Aspects of 'Mormon Westerns.' " *Western American Literature* 8, 1973.

Boal, Sam. "Zane Grey . . . Writer of the Purple Sage." *Coronet,* June 1954.

Boyle, R. H. "The Man Who Lived Two Lives in One." *Sports Illustrated,* 29 April 1968.

Cawelti, John. "God's Country, Las Vegas, and the Gun Fighter: Differing Visions of the West." *Western American Literature* 9, February 1975.

———. "The Gunfighter and Society." *American West* 5, March 1968.

———. "Savagery, Civilization and the Western Hero." In *Focus on the Western.* Edited by Jack Nachbar. Englewood Cliffs, N.J.: Prentice-Hall, 1974.

Cleland, E., and E. "House That Grey Built." *Arizona Wildlife Sportsman,* May 1953.

Dedera, D. "Shame of the Rim Now Its Showcase." *Arizona Days and Ways,* 29 March 1964.

Early, Elinor. "He Made the West Famous." *True West,* March 1969.

Elkin, Frederick. "The Psychological Appeal for Children of the Hollywood B Western." In *Focus on the Western.* Edited by Jack Nachbar. Englewood Cliffs, N.J.: Prentice-Hall, 1974.

Etulain, Richard W. "Cultural Origins of the Western." In *Focus on the Western.* Edited by Jack Nachbar. Englewood Cliffs, N.J.: Prentice-Hall, 1974.

———. "A Dedication to the Memory of Zane Grey." *Arizona and the West* 12, Autumn 1970.

Farley, G. M. "Zane Grey and the Great Outdoors." *Zane Grey Western* 5, 1973.

———. "Zane Grey, Man of the West." *Real West,* September 1972.

———. "Zane Grey's Arizona." *Zane Grey Collector* 4, 1971.

———. "Zane Grey's Fight with Arizona." *Zane Grey Collector* 4, 1971.

Folsom, James K. "Westerns as Social and Political Alternatives." In *Focus on the Western.* Edited by Jack Nachbar. Englewood Cliffs, N.J.: Prentice-Hall, 1974.

Goble, Danny. "The Days That Were No More: A Look at Zane Grey's West." *Journal of Arizona History* 14, Spring 1973.

"Goettle's Zane Grey Cabin." *Tonto Trails,* Summer 1981.

Hayden, Mike. "Fishing Zane Grey's River." *Field and Stream,* October 1962.

Helminiak, Raymond. "The About-Face of a Buffalo Hunter." *Frontier Times,* November 1971.

"Heroes Ride on Forever." *Time,* 19 June 1950.

Homans, Peter. "Puritanism Revisited: An Analysis of the Contemporary Screen Image Western." In *Focus on the Western.* Edited by Jack Nachbar. Englewood Cliffs, N.J.: Prentice-Hall, 1974.

Hough, Donald. "The Great Kaibab Deer Drive." *Zane Grey Collector* 4, 1971.

Kemp, D. "Writer, Sportsman, Arizona's First Ambassador . . . Zane Grey." *Phoenix,* February 1969.

Kimball, Ethel. "Trail to Thunder Mountain." *True West,* March 1973.

Kitses, Jim. "The Western: Ideology and Archetype." In *Focus on the Western.* Edited by Jack Nachbar. Englewood Cliffs, N.J.: Prentice-Hall, 1974.

Mead, Norman W. "Zane Grey, the Man Whose Books Made the West Famous Lived Here." *Arizona Highways,* October 1973.

Moses, Montrose J. "Zane Grey, Literary Craftsman." *The Book News Monthly,* February 1918.

Netherby, Steve. "Zane Grey: Author, Angler, and Explorer." *Field and Stream,* January 1972.

"New York's Awe at the Best Seller." *The Literary Digest,* 10 March 1923.

"Obituary." *Publisher's Weekly,* 28 October 1939.

"Obituary." *Newsweek,* 30 October 1939.

Olsen, T. V. "Zane Grey: How He Grew." *The Roundup,* September 1966.

———. "Zane Grey: The Writer and His West." *The Roundup,* October 1966.

Peeples, Samuel A. "Zane Grey: The Man Who Influenced Me Most." *Zane Grey Collector* 4, 1971.

Peplow, Edward H. J. "The Legend of Pearl Grey." *Arizona Highways,* April 1966.

"Pre-Beowulf." *Time,* 16 May 1938.

"Return of Zane Grey." *Newsweek,* 12 September 1955.

Roberts, Gary L. "The West's Gunmen, Part I." *American West* 8, January 1971.

———. "The West's Gunmen, Part II." *American West* 8, March 1971.

Scheff, V. "A Visit with Zane Grey." *Outdoor Arizona,* April 1973.

Schubert, Paul. "Roundup in Bloody Basin." *The Saturday Evening Post,* 15 February 1958.

Stanley, R. "Legacy from Lo-Lomai." *Westways,* May 1956.

Stocker, Joseph. "Zane Grey and Pleasant Valley." *Westways,* February 1960.

"The Talk of the Town." *The New Yorker,* 19 July 1952.

Tallon, James. "Zane Grey's Rim: Coconino and Sitgreaves National Forests, Arizona." *Travel,* June 1975.

Topping, Gary. "Zane Grey's West." *Journal of Popular Culture* 7, Winter, 1973.

Tuska, Jon. "The American Western Cinema: 1903–Present." In *Focus on the Western.* Edited by Jack Nachbar. Englewood Cliffs, N.J.: Prentice-Hall, 1974.

Woody, Clara T., and Milton L. Schwartz. "War in Pleasant Valley: The Outbreak of the Graham-Tewksbury Feud." *The Journal of Arizona History* 18, 1977.